THE BEST
DOG TRICKS
★ ON THE PLANET ★

THE BEST
DOG TRICKS
★ ON THE PLANET ★

★ 106 AMAZING THINGS ★
YOUR DOG CAN DO ON COMMAND

BABETTE HAGGERTY
CELEBRITY DOG TRAINER AND HEAD OF THE HAGGERTY SCHOOL FOR DOGS

WITH BARBARA CALL

★ ★ ★

PAGE STREET
PUBLISHING CO.

First published in 2013 by

Page Street Publishing Co.

27 Congress Street, Suite 103

Salem, MA 01970

www.pagestreetpublishing.com

Distributed by Macmillan; sales in Canada by The Canadian Manda Group; distribution in Canada by The Jaguar Book Group.

16   15   14   13   1   2   3   4   5

ISBN-13: 978-1-62414-004-4

ISBN-10: 1-62414-004-1

Library of Congress Control Number: 2013942547

Cover and book design by Page Street Publishing Co.

Photography by Tamara Lee-Sang

Printed and bound in U.S.A

Page Street is proud to be a member of 1% for the Planet. Members donate one percent of their sales to one or more of the over 1,500 environmental and sustainability charities across the globe who participate in this program.

★ FOR MY DAD ★

★ CONTENTS ★

★ INTRODUCTION ★

Our relationship with dogs has evolved as the modern world has evolved. Dogs have moved from the backyard to our feet by the hearth, to our offices, to strollers as we walk down the street. Dogs need us and we need them. They not only provide companionship and learn tasks such as finding lost keys, but they also alert diabetics to attacks, comfort those who are sick, rescue people and even help rehabilitate prisoners who find jobs as dog walkers and trainers.

Trick training isn't just for entertainment or creating a helper or even for making sure you've got a polite and well-socialized dog. Trick training creates a strong bond between you and your pet. That means, at its base, trick training can turn everyday dogs into once-in-a-lifetime dogs. Doesn't everyone want that once-in-a-lifetime dog? I do!

You may ask, why another trick book? Today, it seems like everyone is a dog trainer, but not everyone works the same way or with the same techniques. I apply several key concepts to my work as a trainer and to the tricks in this book.

First, I believe dogs, like kids, thrive on boundaries. They appreciate knowing what is expected of them. Dogs that know boundaries are happier, more confident and more relaxed.

Second, I believe in using a clicker, a dog-training concept that dates back to the 1900s. Like all tools, it has its place; misuse or overuse of any tool can create problems. Everything in moderation, and this is true with your clicker. There are times I will use a clicker to mark a behavior and other times I will use verbal praise instead. The clicker is useful for marking a correct behavior at the exact second the dog is doing it. Verbal praise is especially beneficial if you don't have a free hand for a clicker. The verbal praise and clicker both help the dog connect the behavior with the reward.

Perhaps most importantly, I believe in balance. I believe that dogs learn most efficiently when you teach them to do something correctly and you correct them when they do something wrong.

Correcting in trick training and correcting in obedience training are different. In obedience training, correcting means telling a dog, "no." Experience has taught me that ignoring bad behavior does not extinguish it. Correcting it fairly and firmly does. If your dog jumps, barks or even bites, you can't ignore it. You've got to firmly and fairly teach your dog, "No, that's a bad idea."

When trick training, correcting means stopping the behavior, telling them no and then showing them the correct way.

So what does this all mean? When you read this book, you will see lots of treats and clickers. Lots of love and praise will go even further. And remember, it is okay to say "no" to your dog. They will still love you, I promise.

Most important? HAVE FUN. Your dog wants to please you and he wants to have fun, too. The more you embrace the concept of trick training as adventure, the more likely you'll have a good time and find success at creating your once-in-a-lifetime dog!

Happy training!
Babette

CHAPTER ONE

BUILDING BLOCKS

Ready, set, go! You and Rover are about to set off on a fun and exciting adventure that will bring the two of you closer together and give you plenty of fodder for entertaining your friends and family!

Every successful adventure requires planning, practicing and preparing. You wouldn't set out to join the circus without learning to fly on a trapeze or juggle, right? So it is with dog training and obedience. Before you can successfully jump into teaching your dog most of the tricks in this book, you need a strong set of behavioral fundamentals in place. A dog that sits, stays, comes and so on is a well-socialized dog, a dog other people will be comfortable around and a dog that's ready to learn.

This chapter teaches fundamental building-block commands. Once your dog has mastered these tricks, meaning he can do them reliably and consistently with voice and/or hand commands alone, you'll be prepared for the adventure ahead. Practice makes perfect, too. In the same way that you'd practice walking on a tightrope before performing in front of an audience, practicing the building-block commands, even once you and your dog are off and running, is essential. If Rover starts to get sloppy or cut corners, revisiting the fundamentals is critical.

Let's not forget adventures are supposed to be fun! A big part of your and your dog's success in learning anything involves having a good time. Tap into your dog's natural enthusiasm for playing and pleasing you and you're halfway there. Let's get started!

★ SIT ★

Just about every dog knows how to sit, even young puppies! Teaching your dog Sit is quick and easy. Any dog can master this basic training in just a few hours, provided you use the correct technique.

⊕ **HAND SIGNAL**
🐾 **VERBAL CUE:** "Sit"
⚙ **TOOLS:** Praise
🕐 **AVG. TIME:** 3-5 Days
✚ **DIFFICULTY:** Beginner

STEP-BY-STEP

1. Place your dog next to you, on your left-hand side.

2. Turn slightly towards him and bring his muzzle up with your right hand under his chin; his nose should end up pointing to the sky. Caress his back with your left hand. Move your left hand towards his hindquarters and tell him, "Sit."

3. If your dog resists, just hold steady. As you are placing him into this position, you are shifting his weight, which helps place him into a sitting position.

4. As soon as he sits, give him lots of love and praise. Your hands are already on him so the timing for your praise will be perfect. Practice six to eight times a day for three to five days.

 ADVICE FROM THE EXPERT

Contrary to common thinking, pushing your dog's rear end down isn't the best way to teach Sit. Instead? Teach him to shift his weight, which is the natural movement towards a seated position.

 **PROBLEM SOLVING**

Problem: Your dog isn't responding.

Solution: Beware of repeating the Sit command over and over. Instead, back up and repeat the steps. Tell the dog to sit once and only once. Make eye contact and use a firm voice.

★ STAY ★

- ◉ **HAND SIGNAL**
- ✌ **VERBAL CUE:** "Stay"
- ✿ **TOOLS:** Praise
- ◷ **AVG. TIME:** 3-5 Days
- ✚ **DIFFICULTY:** Beginner

Teaching Stay is important and not just because it's the opposite of Come (page 12). A dog that stays is a dog that's listening and that's the key for success in all training situations. Stay is combined with other commands for Sit-Stay (step 8 below), Stand-Stay (step 9 below) and Down-Stay (Down, step 5, page 15).

STEP-BY-STEP

1. Put your dog on the leash and have him Sit. Stand in the heel position (sidebar, page 12). Place a flat hand in front of his face and tell him, "Stay."

2. Slowly swing around to stand in front of him, blocking any forward motion with your left leg. Tell him, "Stay" and show him your hand signal.

3. Slowly back away, one step at a time, telling him, "Staaaaayyyy." As you back up, slowly let the leash out.

4. If he gets up, step in quickly, pick up the leash and say, "No. Staaaayyyyy."

5. Start moving in towards him. When you get close to him, put your left hand on his left cheek and slowly circle around behind him.

6. As you circle around behind him, make certain that you maintain eye contact and constant contact with his cheek. This keeps him staying put, and you keep the praise coming while he stays.

7. Once you come all the way back into Heel position, release and give him lots of love and praise.

8. Practice three to five times a day. By day five your dog should have the trick down pat. Then move on to the two commands to teach him Sit-Stay.

9. Similar steps can be taken to teach the dog Stand-Stay. There is no specific Stand position; the goal is simply to have the dog standing in place.

🏅 ADVICE FROM THE EXPERT

Your dog follows your body language. This is a trick that requires a calm, relaxed posture. Use a firm but quieter tone instead of your happy, energetic voice. Keep in mind that Stay is the opposite of what just about every dog wants to do, so a relaxed stance and calm voice is essential.

- ⊕ **HAND SIGNAL**
- ☝ **VERBAL CUE:** "Come"
- ⚙ **TOOLS:** Praise
- ⏱ **AVG. TIME:** 3-5 Days
- ✚ **DIFFICULTY:** Beginner

★ COME ★

Come is one of the most important obedience commands. I'm sure you can think of situations where you need your dog to Come in order to stay safe or avoid conflict. I don't recommend issuing Come with your dog off the leash until he's completely reliable responding to Come on the leash in an enclosed area.

STEP-BY-STEP

1. Work in a fenced area where your dog can't run off or get easily distracted. Place your dog on the leash. Have him Sit-Stay (Stay, step 8, page 11). Hold onto the leash, walk to the end of the leash and turn to face him.

2. Place your left arm out to the side and bring it to your right shoulder. As you do that, in a happy voice say, "Come."

3. As he comes over, start backing up, even breaking into a little backwards jog, encouraging him to follow you.

4. Once he gets to you, give him lots and lots of praise.

5. Practice three to five times a day; by day five your dog should come on command.

TEACHING YOUR DOG TO HEEL

Start with your dog on a leash and sitting on your left side. Pat your thigh so it makes a slapping noise (eventually he will associate that sound with Heel) and start walking with your left foot first. Walk at your pace, not the dog's pace. Say, "Heel, good dog" every few seconds in a calm voice while slapping your thigh. Use the leash as needed to keep him on your left side and keep his attention.

Practice this several times a day for a week. Remember to correct Rover if he starts to drift away or becomes distracted.

🦴 PROBLEM SOLVING

Problem: Your dog is distracted and wants to go elsewhere.

Solution: Use his name to get his attention and use your happy voice. If this doesn't work, don't let him get away with it. You need to follow through and give him a leash correction (above).

★ DROP IT ★

Drop It is an important obedience command, not just so you can play throw-and-retrieve the stick, but also in case Rover picks up something he shouldn't (a glove or slipper) or even something dangerous (a chocolate bunny). Have patience and use lots of praise. If your dog values the item you're asking him to drop, remember it's his natural tendency to hold onto it. Dogs can be very possessive!

⊙ HAND SIGNAL
℞ VERBAL CUE: "Drop it"
✿ TOOLS: Praise and Clicker
⊙ AVG. TIME: 5-7 Days
✛ DIFFICULTY: Beginner

STEP-BY-STEP

1. Put your dog on the leash and give him a stick or toy. Tell him, "Drop It." When he won't let go of it, give a little tug on the leash and tell him, "Drop it."

2. If he still won't Drop It, correct him more strongly.

3. Once he spits it out, you can click and give him lots of praise.

4. Repeat three to five times a day for five to seven days.

ADVICE FROM THE EXPERT

Don't be tentative when teaching this trick. Be firm, say, "Drop it" once, and use a calm voice. Be gentle; not aggressive, but assertive. After all, you're the boss.

🦴 PROBLEM SOLVING

Problem: Your dog won't let go of the object.
Solution: Cradle his muzzle firmly but gently in your right hand and say, "Drop it." If this doesn't work, you can pry his mouth open with your left hand and take the object out of his mouth. Then start over with the step-by-step training sequence.

Problem: Your dog drops the object, but when you reach down to pick it up he lunges in and grabs it.
Solution: This has to be corrected, not only to show him that it's not allowed, but also because you or someone else might get nipped by accident when he tries to grab the object. To correct him, put him in a Sit-Stay (Stay, step 9, page 11) and use a firm voice to tell him, "No." Then start over with the step-by-step, but put him into a Sit-Stay before you ask him to drop it until he masters the concept. Be patient. Learning to curb his enthusiasm and calmly sit down may take time!

★ DOWN ★

- **HAND SIGNAL**
- **VERBAL CUE:** "Down"
- **TOOLS:** Praise and Treats
- **AVG. TIME:** 3-5 Days
- **DIFFICULTY:** Beginner

Teaching Rover Down taps into his natural need for resting and sleeping, something all dogs do, especially after big excursions. Mastering this trick also means your dog knows who is boss (you). Last but not least, this obedience command is the building block for a variety of fun tricks later in the book, including Dead Dog (page 17) and Roll Over (page 58).

STEP-BY-STEP

1. Start your dog in Sit. Take a treat and show it to him in your hand.

2. Starting above his head, bring your closed hand down past his face, then put the treat on the ground. As you do this, tell him, "Dooooowwwwwnnn."

Show the dog the treat as you move your hand to the ground.

3. As he follows your hand, wait until he is all the way down before you give him the treat.

4. If he brings his rear end up, just wait him out, keeping your hand on the ground, waiting for him to go down. Once he goes down give him the treat and lots of praise.

5. After he's mastered Down, add Stay (page 11) to teach Down-Stay. Build up to longer periods of time in the Down-Stay position before rewarding him.

6. Practice three to five times a day for three to five days.

Reward him with the treat and lots of praise.

ADVICE FROM THE EXPERT

Practice makes perfect. Down and Down-Stay are perfect examples of where you can build success with repetition. Start by having your dog stay down for one minute, then two minutes, and so on. Eventually build up to thirty minutes in Down-Stay. You can check your email while he waits!

PROBLEM SOLVING

Problem: Your dog's crouching above the ground, ready to jump up.

Solution: Use a calm and firm tone to tell him, "Down." If he's sitting Sphinx-like stroke his back to help him relax and release.

Problem: Your dog pops up from the Down position as soon as you reward him with a treat.

Solution: If you've got a very food-focused pup then use praise as the reward instead of food.

★ SPEAK ★

HAND SIGNAL
VERBAL CUE: "Speak"
TOOLS: Praise and Treats
AVG. TIME: 5-7 Days
DIFFICULTY: Intermediate

Most dogs bark, sometimes for protection and other times out of excitement. Take note of what excites your dog. Is it hunger? The words "go for a walk"? Tap into his enthusiasm and your success is practically guaranteed! Once Rover has mastered Speak you can move to a whole assortment of fun and useful tricks, such as Bark to Go Out (page 60) and the entertaining Do Your Arithmetic (page 119).

STEP-BY-STEP

1. Hold a treat in front of Rover and teasingly say, "Speak, speak!"

2. Let him get excited and once he barks, even a half bark, tell him, "Good dog!" and give him the treat as well as lots of love and praise.

3. Practice three to five times a day for five to seven days. Every time he barks (e.g., for the doorbell, at another dog) tell him, "Speak, good boy, speak!"

ADVICE FROM THE EXPERT

This is easier to teach with a hungry dog, as you're more likely to get him to bark!

PROBLEM SOLVING

Problem: Your dog isn't a natural barker.

Solution: Here's my method for encouraging him to speak. Use the leash to tie him to a post or handrail. Stay a few feet away, longer than the leash length, and tease him. Dangle his favorite treat, but make sure he can't get to you. Being restrained will antagonize and frustrate him, making him more likely to use his vocal chords! If Rover gives you even a fraction of a sound, whether it's a whine, a bark or a friendly growl, give him lots of praise, click, treat and say, "Good dog."

★ DEAD DOG ★

HAND SIGNAL
VERBAL CUE: "Dead dog"
TOOLS: Praise
AVG. TIME: 5-7 Days
DIFFICULTY: Beginner

I once trained a dog whose owner advised the Republican Party. I taught his dog to play Dead Dog whenever my client would ask, "Would you rather be a Democrat or a dead Republican?" This is a fun trick to learn. Once your pup has it mastered, use your imagination to create a script that will get your friends laughing!

STEP-BY-STEP

1. Get Rover into the Down position (page 14). Start stroking him so he relaxes. Stroke along his side telling him, "Dead dog, stay, dead dog, stay."

2. Keep calmly telling him this as you lightly stroke him along his side and gently push him to lie down on his side. The more you practice this the longer he will stay. Once he's lying on his side give him lots of praise. Refrain from using treats as a reward because you don't want to excite him.

3. Practice three to five times a day for five to seven days.

ADVICE FROM THE EXPERT

Your dog needs a solid Down-Stay (Down step 5, page 15) for this trick, so practice until he'll stay in the Down position for at least five minutes. Make sure it's a true Down with hips askew, not sitting up in a Sphinx-like position.

Once you've mastered this trick, try stitching together a full skit. You can set up a funny military scenario: Duck and Cover (page 89), Army Crawl (page 88), play Dead Dog (this trick) and even On Your Back (page 26).

PROBLEM SOLVING

Problem: Your dog won't roll over onto his side.

Solution: Rover needs to be very relaxed to learn this trick, so start by quieting your tone and body language. Make sure your environment is free of distractions—no ringing doorbells or cell phones to rev him up!

★ SIT PRETTY ★

⊕ HAND SIGNAL

♋ VERBAL CUE: "Paw up, Sit pretty"

✿ TOOLS: Praise and Treats

⏲ AVG. TIME: 7-8 Days

✚ DIFFICULTY: Intermediate

Sit Pretty has great entertainment value on its own and serves as the backbone for many other tricks. It also helps you stay in close physical contact with your dog and uses that contact as the reward. Once he Sits Pretty on his own, you can toss him a little treat!

STEP-BY-STEP

1. Start with your dog in Sit (page 10). Hold a treat in front of him.

2. Raise your knee up, raise the treat up, and tell him, "Paws up" (sidebar page 19). The goal is for him to place his front paws onto your knee.

Have your dog sit in front of you while you hold a treat in your hand.

Bring your knee up and move the treat upwards.

3. Once he can consistently do Paws Up to your knee, get behind him and stand in a Charlie Chaplin stance, with your heels touching and feet facing out. Position your dog between your feet, keep your heels touching, and tell him, "Sit."

4. Gently place your hand under Rover's rib cage and start moving his body up to you, so his front paws are off the ground. Keep him in that position for just a few seconds, saying, "Sit pretty." Repeat over a few days to slowly build up his muscles to where he can hold the position for longer periods of time. Give him lots of love and praise as you use your hands to reward and massage him.

5. Transition to holding his paws up in front of you and saying, "Sit pretty."

6. Last, encourage your dog get into the Sit Pretty position on his own. Reward him with a treat.

7. Practice three to five times a day for seven to eight days. This will come easier to some dogs than others.

Tell him "Paws up" to move his paws onto your knee.

Stand behind him as he builds the muscle strength to sit alone.

⚜ ADVICE FROM THE EXPERT

Keep in mind that the alignment of your dog's legs, body and head are essential to his ability to balance. Move away from him very slowly and carefully before you leave him sitting alone.

PAWS UP

1. Sit in a chair with your knees at the right height for your dog's paws or find a table that is appropriate for your dog's height. If you have a small dog you can use an ottoman.

2. Tap your knees or the table and tell your dog, "Paws up." Encourage him up, and as soon as he puts his paws up, give him a treat and praise him.

3. Do this six to ten times the first time, then repeat two to three times for a few days. You won't need to repeat this many times for your dog to reliably respond.

★ WALK ON HIND LEGS ★

Everybody loves a dancing dog and this trick showcases your pup's happy attitude! The great thing about Walk on Hind Legs is where you can take it after your dog has it mastered: Pirouette (page 80), Walk on Hind Legs Forward and Backward (page 78) and Push a Carriage (page 82).

⊕ **HAND SIGNAL**
🖑 **VERBAL CUE:** "Dance"
⚙ **TOOLS:** Praise and Treats
🕐 **AVG. TIME:** 10-14 Days
➕ **DIFFICULTY:** Intermediate

STEP-BY-STEP

1. Hold the treat in front of Rover's nose and slowly bring it up. Watch him to determine how quickly and how high to bring it up. Bring it up slowly enough that he can take it from your hand and not so high that he has to bend his head back to get it. If you bring it up over his head and he jumps, then it's too high.

Hold the treat in front of your dog's nose. Slowly move the treat upward.

Encourage him up onto his hind legs using the treat.

2. Hold the treat just high enough that he comes up on his back legs. If he needs to balance his front legs on you initially that's okay, but slowly move away from him over time, making him balance on his own for longer and longer periods of time. Reward him with the treat and praise.

3. This is a trick that you should work on for just a few moments each day and slowly build up the time he spends on his hindquarters so he can build muscular strength. He should have it nailed within ten to fourteen days.

🏅 ADVICE FROM THE EXPERT

Don't move the treat around too much. You'll want to take note of how high your dog can stand up and feel comfortable.

🦴 PROBLEM SOLVING

Problem: Your dog lunges up to get the treat instead of coming up and holding the position on his back legs.

Solution: Let him brace his paws on your chest or arm if needed, then bring the treat in line with his mouth. Let him nibble at it out of your hand while he's learning to balance.

Reward the upward movement!

★ TOUCH IT ★

Touch It is a simple trick that can be combined with other tricks to create an entertaining skit. Once your dog has mastered the command, use your imagination, look around your home and yard and think about what Rover can "touch" that's typically not associated with doggie behavior or that a dog paw can't easily master. Change up the command for a good laugh! Some of my favorite examples: "Rover, where's my favorite chair?" (teach him to touch the chair) and "Are you ready for your manicure?" (teach him to touch your outstretched hand).

⊕ HAND SIGNAL
✌ VERBAL CUE: "Touch it"
✿ TOOLS: Clicker and Treats
① AVG. TIME: 5-7 Days
✛ DIFFICULTY: Beginner

STEP-BY-STEP

1. Most dogs will paw at you when they want something: a treat, to go outside or to be touched. When Rover paws at you, tell him, "Touch it," then click and treat. It is that simple. When he paws at you or anything else from this point forward, tell him, "Touch it."

2. It will take time for your dog to learn to do this on command. Once he starts pawing on command with some reliability, you can teach him to touch specific objects. Start with your hand. Show your dog the palm of your hand and tell him, "Touch it."

3. Build from there by showing him what you want him to touch, such as the light switch, and say, "Touch it."

4. Once he gets the concept, practice with different objects three to five times a day for five to seven days.

 ADVICE FROM THE EXPERT

This trick is best taught by capturing your dog in action, so be sure to carry your clicker with you at all times. Consistency is key in teaching a trick where you're capturing the action. It's also essential to click at exactly the right second. Practice makes perfect for you and your dog.

 **PROBLEM SOLVING**

Problem: Your dog doesn't really use his paws.

Solution: Some dogs are more paw-oriented than others. You can gently hold his paw and make a pawing motion, then click and treat.

★ TUG IT ★

Tug It is another fun trick that's easy to teach because it taps into your dog's hardwiring. Think back to wild dogs fighting over a scrap of food and you can imagine your dog tugging to his heart's content! The perfect way to start training Tug It is to use a rope toy or an old towel with knots tied in it.

⊙ **HAND SIGNAL**
ℬ **VERBAL CUE:** "Tug"
⚙ **TOOLS:** Praise and Treats
⏲ **AVG. TIME:** 5-7 Days
➕ **DIFFICULTY:** Beginner

STEP-BY-STEP

1. Swing the rope toy or towel around your dog's head and tease him with it until he grabs it. Once he grabs it, tug gently. If you pull too hard he may let go. Repeat.

2. Once Rover starts to really hold on to it and give it a good tug, keep pulling, but then let him win. Rover wins when he starts pulling back a little. Praise him.

3. Go back and forth playing tug, telling him, "Tug, tug." When you want him to let go, pause and tell him, "Drop it" (page 13). If he doesn't let go right away, stick your fingers about halfway between his front and back teeth and pry open his mouth. Tell him, "Drop it" again and once he releases the rope give him a treat.

4. Repeat three to five times a day for five to seven days.

 ADVICE FROM THE EXPERT

Don't pull too hard on the object he's tugging. You've got to let him win a little bit, or even win completely once in a while! If it's not fun he'll eventually lose interest.

There's an old wives' tale that says playing tug will teach your dog to be aggressive. That's nonsense. Almost all dogs enjoy a game of tug! It is important, however, that you teach your dog to stop tugging on command.

★ FIND IT ★

● **HAND SIGNAL**
ॐ **VERBAL CUE:** "Find it"
✿ **TOOLS:** Praise and Treats
🕐 **AVG. TIME:** 5-7 Days
✚ **DIFFICULTY:** Intermediate

Find It taps into Rover's natural inclination to find things. Dogs are hardwired to hunt, regardless of their breed. Combine that instinct with his desire to please you and you can have a lot of fun. It's especially entertaining to teach your dog to find things that are hidden to your friends and guests, such as a pair of eyeglasses carefully planted in someone's purse. Surprise your guests by announcing, "I lost my keys!" and having Rover save the day!

You can also use a technique similar to the game of hot-and-cold. As he gets closer to the object, encourage him in the right direction using the command, "You're getting warmer" in your happy, enthusiastic voice. If he veers off course, use the command, "You're getting colder—go find _____!"

STEP-BY-STEP

1. Start by placing your dog in a Sit-Stay (Stay, step 8, page 11). Create a trail of tiny treats and tell him, "Find it." Let him follow the trail, all the while telling him, "Find it" and encouraging him.

Create a trail of treats.

Use the command "Find it."

Continue cuing with "Find it."

2. Once he finishes the trail and the treats, give him lots of praise.

3. Repeat the process several times. Each time you do it, make the trail a bit more complicated, placing the treats in different rooms. Start with a straight line and gradually weave the trail. Once he starts actively using his nose to find the treats, begin moving the treats to higher ground, such as on the shelves of a bookcase, and placing them farther apart.

4. Practice three to five times a day for five to seven days.

Reward him once he's found all the treats.

ADVICE FROM THE EXPERT

Make sure you use short paths as you train this trick. Start with a 3 foot/0.9-m path of treats, followed by 10 feet/3 m, 15 feet/4.6 m, and so on. Don't start with 30 yards/27.4 m right from the get-go.

PROBLEM SOLVING

Problem: Your dog doesn't seem interested in finding the object.

Solution: Make sure you've got enough treats along the trail and that you're using the right kind of treat, especially if your dog is a picky eater.

Problem: Your dog starts the training but gets distracted or loses focus.

Solution: Make sure you use something he really cares about, something he really wants to find, whether that's his favorite toy, a piece of hot dog or even a ham sandwich!

Problem: Your dog just doesn't seem to grasp the concept of Find It.

Solution: Try working on this trick without training it. Drop a treat or a piece of cheese on the floor and say, "Find it." This will reinforce the concept at a very basic level, and then you're ready to move onto full training.

★ ON YOUR BACK ★

Here's a trick that progresses naturally from Down (page 14) and Dead Dog (page 17). Have Rover roll right onto his back! You can combine the three tricks for a seamless move, or stitch together a skit that involves multiple happy dog moves, such as Wag Your Tail (page 63) and Chase Your Tail (page 130)!

⊙ HAND SIGNAL
℘ VERBAL CUE: "On your back"
✿ TOOLS: Praise
🕐 AVG. TIME: 5-7 Days
✛ DIFFICULTY: Intermediate

STEP-BY-STEP

1. Place your dog into a Down-Stay (page 15), then tell him, "Down, dead dog" (Down, page 14; Dead Dog, page 17).

2. With the back of your hand and a light touch of your fingers, stroke his belly as you tell him, "On your back."

3. As he relaxes, start scratching his belly. The more he relaxes, the more he'll show his belly and turn on his back. Gently repeat, "On your back, on your back."

4. Give him lots of praise when you are ready to release him. Refrain from using treats as a reward for this because you don't want to excite him.

5. Practice three to five times a day for five to seven days.

🏅 ADVICE FROM THE EXPERT

Your dog has to be relaxed to succeed at this trick, and he needs to trust you. This is the most vulnerable position your dog has, so give him lots of praise when he obeys you.

🦴 PROBLEM SOLVING

Problem: Your dog rolls onto his back but then pops right up.

Solution: He's not completely relaxed or he's not comfortable staying in the vulnerable position. Try teaching this trick at night when he's tired or more relaxed. As with many other tricks, you can always break it into pieces and master each section before you put it all together.

★ BUMP ★

HAND SIGNAL
VERBAL CUE: "Bump"
TOOLS: Clicker, Praise and Treats
AVG. TIME: 5-7 Days
DIFFICULTY: Beginner

Remember the Bump, that popular dance move from the '70s? Here's the doggie-style variation. Rover will use his nose rather than his hip! This is one of those tricks that requires catching your dog in action, then clicking and attaching a verbal cue. Once he's mastered Bump use your imagination to create your own entertaining variations, such as "Show me what shoes to wear!" or "Can you close the cupboard door for me?"

STEP-BY-STEP

1. A dog will often nudge you when you are sitting in a chair. When he does say, "Bump" while touching your nose, then click and treat. Repeat three to five times. Click each time and give him lots of praise, followed by the Bump verbal cue.

2. If your dog doesn't automatically nudge you, hide a treat in your hand and hold it by your side to elicit a nudge. When he does, say, "Bump," then click and treat. Repeat three to five times. Click each time and give him lots of praise, followed by the Bump verbal cue.

3. Advance to teaching him to bump objects, such as a small ball. Tell him, "Bump the ball." This teaches him Bump and increases his vocabulary of objects. From there you can move on to other familiar and/or everyday objects.

4. Practice three to five times a day for five to seven days.

ADVICE FROM THE EXPERT
Some dogs will catch on to Bump right away. The training here really involves identifying the object to touch with his nose. If your dog needs help learning to identify the object, skip ahead to Name That Thingamajig (page 33).

PROBLEM SOLVING
Problem: Your dog over-bumps, constantly nudging your hand so you'll pet him.

Solution: This isn't really a big deal. Just ignore him and eventually he'll learn you're not going to respond every single time.

★ HUP ★

- ⊕ **HAND SIGNAL**
- ⌥ **VERBAL CUE:** "Hup"
- ⚙ **TOOLS:** Praise and Treats
- ⌚ **AVG. TIME:** 3-5 Days
- ✚ **DIFFICULTY:** Beginner

Teach Rover to Hup (jump) and you're set up for a whole assortment of entertaining tricks, from Pony Ride (page 146) to Jump over Another Dog (page 94) to Jump through My Arms (page 168). I'm sure you can imagine any number of ways to create an entertaining trick of your own using Hup. How about asking Rover to jump into the lawn chair after he brings you a bottled water at the neighborhood cookout (Fetch, page 31; Name That Thingamajig, page 33)?

More advanced tricks using Hup include jumping onto a big circus-style ball, jumping rope, or even jumping onto a moving object such as a wagon your kids are pulling or a wheelbarrow you're using to work in the yard. Hup also has everyday applications, as in, "Hup into the car."

If your dog cannot already jump, sit cross-legged and pat your chest.

STEP-BY-STEP

1. There are a couple of ways to teach Hup. If your dog already jumps up on your legs, you're halfway there. Just pat your chest, tell him, "Hup," reach down and scoop him up under his hindquarters. Give him a treat and lots of praise.

2. If your dog does not jump up on your legs then sit cross-legged on the floor. Call your dog in an excited, happy tone using his name and the Come command (page 12) but not the Come hand signal. Pat your chest at the same time. Keep calling him and patting your chest until he gets all the way into your lap. As he's climbing in your lap say, "Hup," then "Good dog" and give lots of praise.

3. Once he crawls into your lap on command, which takes about three days to learn, repeat the same exercise but say, "Hup!" and pat your chest. Don't say, "Come."

4. Sit in a chair. If your dog is right in front of you say, "Hup!" and pat your chest. Your dog should jump into your lap. Give lots of praise.

5. If he doesn't jump into your lap, put the leash on him and give a gentle tug when you say, "Hup". Practice five to seven times twice a day for three to five days.

Next, sit in a chair and pat your chest.

Move onto having your dog jump into the chair by himself.

6. Once he jumps into your lap consistently, you can get him to Hup into the chair without you in it, into the car or onto the sofa. For example, to get him to Hup into the car put on his leash, place his paws up on the seat of the car, apply a little bit of tension on the leash, and pull him up while giving him a little boost from below. Say, "Hup."

7. Practice this every day for three to five days.

8. During the practice period, if he jumps up on the sofa, your bed or anywhere else he's allowed, take that opportunity and tell him, "Hup."

9. After he masters Hup, you can teach him to Hup into your arms. Crouch down slightly. Pat your chest and say, "Hup." Your dog should jump into your arms. Be ready to catch him!

 ADVICE FROM THE EXPERT

The key to teaching Hup? Be consistent. Use the verbal command every time, but don't be afraid to correct Rover if he jumps onto something he shouldn't without being asked.

PROBLEM SOLVING

Problem: Your dog starts jumping onto things he shouldn't without being asked or given permission.

Solution: If he starts doing this, you've got to use a strong, firm voice and tell him, "No."

Problem: Your dog jumps up onto people.

Solution: This is something that has to be corrected. A polite and well-behaved dog does not jump up, in part because you don't want to knock anyone down, but also to avoid situations like getting his muddy paw prints on your boss's beautiful white skirt! If your dog does this correct him immediately by bringing your leg up like you're marching and firmly and carefully use your knee to knock him off balance. Tell him, "No" in a strong, firm voice.

Crouch down slightly to help your dog jump into your arms.

CHAPTER TWO

FETCH, CATCH AND FIND

Fetch and catch are fun activities for any dog. Although learning Fetch will come more naturally to certain breed such as retrievers, most dogs like to go after things. The action is hardwired into their DNA: Think about how their wild ancestors needed to chase down their prey. Translate that skill to the domesticated dog and voilà! Fetch is an activity that already feels familiar.

Finding things is also hardwired into a dog's DNA. Think of a wolf's must-have survival skill: finding food. Teaching your dog to find something he loves builds on his inherited "find it" ability. Finding already feels familiar to him.

Catch, on the other hand, is pure fun. We all know dogs love to have fun. They also will pick up on your mood if you're having fun, and will want to have fun too.

Although feeling useful seems like a human trait, dogs also love to feel useful. It taps into their natural desire to please you, which manifests in everything from behaving properly to snuggling up when you're feeling down. If you combine that desire with some practical, fun and clever items like slippers, the mail or his leash, you'll have a whole assortment of impressive tricks in your bag!

 # ★ FETCH ★

Retrieving is a fun game, so start this training with enthusiasm! Some dogs will catch on immediately, hence the name "retriever." If you've got a dog that's not a natural-born fetcher, you'll need to be patient and give it time. Don't give up and don't expect overnight results, but if you're firm and consistent all dogs have the potential to become top-notch fetchers.

⊕ HAND SIGNAL
✌ VERBAL CUE: "Fetch"
✿ TOOLS: Clicker and Praise
⏱ AVG. TIME: 5-7 Days
✚ DIFFICULTY: Beginner

STEP-BY-STEP

1. As you play with Rover, throw a stick and say, "Fetch." This will test his retrieving instincts. If he brings it back to you, give him lots of love and praise.

2. Before you throw it again, break the stick in half and rub your hands all over it. Your scent will help him find it. Say, "Fetch" and see if he brings it back.

3. As he holds the stick in his mouth, give him lots of love and praise. Don't worry at this point if he doesn't release the stick. Just let him hold it.

4. Next move to objects. Throw some of his favorite toys and say, "Fetch." If he has a natural instinct to carry the toy in his mouth, click as soon as he puts his mouth on it. If he just sniffs the toy and doesn't carry it, click that as well. If he drops the object and comes over to you, give him lots of praise.

5. Build on this as he continues to move closer to putting a toy in his mouth, then progresses to picking up the toy. Keep saying, "Fetch" and clicking along. As long as he progresses you will click because you are shaping the behavior.

6. Repeat two to three times a day for five to seven days. Once he brings the object to you, you have hit the jackpot!

✪ ADVICE FROM THE EXPERT

Don't push too hard or too long on teaching this trick. Do each stage for four or five minutes each session. If he loses interest, pick up your treats and clicker and go home. It's always important to always end on a high note.

🦴 PROBLEM SOLVING

Problem: Your dog doesn't seem to catch on.

Solution: Work with one toy, and one toy only. This will keep him focused on the task at hand. Then toss the object very close to him, such as 6 inches/15 cm away, not 6 feet/1.8 m. Work slowly to progress from 6 inches/15 cm to 12 inches/ 30.5 cm, 1 foot/0.3 m to 3 feet/0.9 m, 3 feet/0.9 m to 6 feet/ 1.8 m, and so on.

★ CAN YOU ANSWER ★ THE PHONE?

The phone's ringing, but you're in the kitchen scrubbing pots and pans and your hands are wet and soapy. Forget asking your seven-year-old to grab it. Put Rover to work instead. This is a fun and practical trick and it's sure to elicit a laugh from dinner guests and kids alike. Once Rover has mastered the ringing portion of this trick you can teach him different ring tones and call out, "Can you grab that? It's Grandma on the phone!"

⊕ HAND SIGNAL
☏ VERBAL CUE: "Get the phone"
✿ TOOLS: Praise
⏱ AVG. TIME: 5-7 Days
✚ DIFFICULTY: Intermediate

STEP-BY-STEP

1. Start by using the technique outlined in Name that Thingamajig (page 33) to teach Rover to identify a non-ringing phone (landline or cell phone).

2. Practice finding it with the non-ringing phone using the command, "Get the phone!"

3. Teach him to get the ringing phone by saying "Get the phone." Use the same ring tone over and over again so he can identify the ring tone initially. Set up the phone to ring, then bring him over to it and say, "Get the phone, get the phone."

4. Once he picks it up, put out your hand and say, "Drop it" (page 13). Once he reliably gives you the phone, you can drop the Drop It command.

5. Next, teach the dog to bring it to you. Stand away from the phone and the dog and when the phone rings, use the command, "Get the phone, fetch" (page 31). Once the dog reliably retrieves, drop the "fetch."

6. Practice three to five times a day for five to seven days.

> **🏅 ADVICE FROM THE EXPERT**
> Most dogs have what's called a "soft mouth" when carrying something, versus a harder mouth when they are chewing on food. I personally don't worry about letting my dog put his teeth on my phone, but if you've got an unprotected touch screen or you're afraid Rover will chomp down hard you may want to skip this trick.

★ NAME THAT ★ THINGAMAJIG

⊕ HAND SIGNAL
✆ VERBAL CUE: "Get _____"
✿ TOOLS: Praise
⊙ AVG. TIME: 5-7 Days
✚ DIFFICULTY: Beginner

What's the name of that thingamajig? You know, the soft shoes I wear to keep my feet warm? That's right—slippers! Just like you used memory to learn the name of things as a child, you can teach your dog the names of familiar, everyday objects, from his leash to your cell phone. Once he's mastered identifying objects and he's got Fetch (page 31) down pat, you can have a lot of fun. How about teaching Rover to identify your husband's favorite magazine and bring it to him as he plops onto the couch to relax?

STEP-BY-STEP

1. Place a tennis ball in front of Rover and tell him, "Get the ball!" Make sure this is the only object available for him, to avoid confusion. Once he picks it up, give him lots of praise.

2. Repeat this five to eight times until he knows what the ball is, each time giving him lots of praise.

3. Place the ball next to a toy. Give the toy a name, such as Teddy, and tell him, "Get Teddy." If he starts to get the ball, gently tell him, "Noooo, get Teddy." Point to Teddy and encourage him to, "Get Teddy."

4. Once he takes it, give him lots of praise. If he doesn't bring it to you, that's okay. Just praise him for knowing which item you wanted.

5. Practice three to five times a day for five to seven days with one or two objects.

6. When you're ready to move on to other objects, offer Rover the object so he can smell it (every object has a different smell), even lick it, and get to know the object before learning its name.

✪ ADVICE FROM THE EXPERT
Repetition is the key to success in teaching this trick. Work on one toy until he's really good at that toy. Test him by putting that toy in the middle of all the other toys. When he can consistently pick it out then he's ready to add other toys.

BRING ME MY KEYS ★

What dog doesn't love a ride in the car, windows down and ears flapping? Once he learns this trick he can bring you the keys, Hup into the car (page 28) and go for a ride! Start by teaching Rover to identify your keys, then store them in a place he can reach easily, like a low table or basket.

⊕ **HAND SIGNAL**
🖐 **VERBAL CUE:** "Get the keys"
⚙ **TOOLS:** Praise
🕐 **AVG. TIME:** 5-7 Days
✚ **DIFFICULTY:** intermediate

STEP-BY-STEP

1. Place your keys on the floor in front of your dog. Point to your keys and tell him, "Get the keys!" Once he shows interest give him praise.

Point to your keys and encourage your dog to pick them up.

2. Repeat "Get the keys," adding in "Fetch" until he picks up the keys and brings them to you, all the time giving him lots of praise. Continue practicing, eventually weaning off the Fetch command and just using, "Get the keys."

3. For a more advanced version, start hiding your keys in less obvious places, such as under the end table. There's nothing wrong with giving Rover hints and telling him where to find them. Think of the hot-and-cold game. Progress by hiding your keys under the couch cushions or a blanket where he can't see it.

4. Practice three to five times a day for five to seven days.

Once he picks up the keys, praise and practice several times.

 ADVICE FROM THE EXPERT

Your dog has three things to learn here: what the keys are, how to bring them to you, and where to find them if they're hidden or lost. Be sure Rover has mastered each individual step before you attempt stringing them together.

Here's a fun variation on this trick: Teach your dog to find the remote. A friend of mine once told me that if I bought a big-enough TV my boyfriends might last longer. Well, this variation may keep yours around longer, or at least make them realize that your cute little bichon isn't a sissy dog!

PROBLEM SOLVING

Problem: Your 5 pound/2.3-kg Yorkshire terrier can't get his mouth around the keys.

Solution: Tie a soft string or lightweight rope around them and let him drag or carry the bunch of keys.

★ BRING ME A TISSUE ★

This is a hilarious trick that a lot of trainers borrowed from my dad, dog trainer Arthur Haggerty, founder of Haggerty's School for Dogs. It used to catch my father's guests off guard when his German Shepherd, Barkley, appeared like the consummate butler with a tissue after they sneezed!

● **HAND SIGNAL**
🖑 **VERBAL CUE:** "Achoo"
⚙ **TOOLS:** Praise and Treats
🕐 **AVG. TIME:** 5-7 Days
✚ **DIFFICULTY:** Intermediate

STEP-BY-STEP

1. Begin with a tissue box next to you on the floor. Make sure a tissue is sticking up.

Begin with a tissue box next to you on the floor.

2. Tell Rover, "Achoo!" as well as, "Get it" and point to the tissue. Once he grabs the tissue give him a treat and lots of praise. Repeat several times a day for a few days.

3. Build up to telling him, "Achoo, get the tissue, fetch" (Fetch, page 31). Once he retrieves the tissue and brings it to you, transition to just, "Achoo!"

4. Practice several times a day for five to seven days.

Tell Rover, "Achoo!" as well as, "Get it" and point to the tissue.

 ADVICE FROM THE EXPERT

This is an intermediate trick with two main steps involved, so be patient. Make sure Rover's got a solid Fetch in place, then teach him to identify a tissue.

Don't use this trick with any kind of breed that drools a lot or has excessive saliva, such as a bulldog or Newfoundland. Otherwise you'll end up with a big mess!

PROBLEM SOLVING

Problem: Your dog can't grab onto a single tissue.

Solution: It may be easier to twist up the top of a protruding tissue from a pop-up vertical box than to teach him to grab a single tissue.

Once he grabs the tissue give him a treat and lots of praise.

★ BRING ME ★ YOUR FOOD DISH

⊕ HAND SIGNAL
꙰ VERBAL CUE: "Get your food dish"
✿ TOOLS: Praise
⊙ AVG. TIME: 5-7 Days
✛ DIFFICULTY: Intermediate

This trick builds on the enthusiasm most dogs exhibit around dinnertime. I know a rat terrier named Cody who barks, sneezes, dances and wiggles when his owner says, "Want your supper?" This is a great trick for impressing friends at a cookout. Imagine your dog has an empty water dish sitting across the yard. You know he needs a refill, so have him trot over, bring his dish back to you and let the kids fill it with the garden hose! Want to really impress your guests? Teach Rover how to pull the hose off the hose spool (Tug It, page 23)!

STEP-BY-STEP

1. Teach him what his food dish is using the instructions in Name That Thingamajig (page 33). Say, "Get your food dish." Praise him if he gets it, even if he doesn't bring it to you.

2. If he doesn't bring it back to you, use the Fetch command (page 31) to teach him to bring it to you. Say, "Get your food dish, fetch." When he brings it to you, praise him.

3. Once he reliably brings you the food dish, drop "Fetch" and simply use, "Get your food dish."

4. Practice several times a day for five to seven days.

ADVICE FROM THE EXPERT

Be sure to use a lightweight cloth, stainless steel or plastic food dish with an easy-to-grip lip for this trick. I recommend stainless steel as plastic has been shown to contribute to plaque buildup on a dog's teeth.

PROBLEM SOLVING

Problem: Rover knows where his food dish is, but getting him to pick it up and bring it to you is a different matter.

Solution: As with most of these "go get it and bring it to me" tricks you'll need a solid Fetch (page 31) in place. Relearn that command and practice until you're sure your dog has it mastered.

★ GET YOUR LEASH ★

We all know Rover loves the phrase, "Want your supper?" Chances are pretty high he loves the phrase, "Want to go for a walk?" as much or even more! Tap into this natural enthusiasm to teach this trick and you'll have a very happy dog. Not surprisingly, this trick is taught in a very similar sequence to "Bring Me Your Food Dish" (page 38).

⊕ HAND SIGNAL
✌ VERBAL CUE: "Get your leash"
✿ TOOLS: Praise
◔ AVG. TIME: 5-7 Days
✛ DIFFICULTY: Intermediate

STEP-BY-STEP

1. Teach him what his leash is using Name That Thingamajig (page 33). Say, "Get your leash." Praise him if he gets it, even if he doesn't bring it to you.

2. If he doesn't bring it to you, use the Fetch command (page 31) to teach him. Say, "Get your leash, fetch." When he brings it to you, praise him.

3. Once he reliably brings you the leash, drop "Fetch" and simply use, "Get your leash."

4. Practice several times a day for five to seven days.

 ADVICE FROM THE EXPERT

Get Your Leash is just the start of a whole collection of tricks you can teach Rover regarding his own stuff. Start with his leash then move on to his collar (assuming he's not wearing it), his harness, even his winter coat!

PROBLEM SOLVING

Problem: He's got his leash, but he wants to play tug of war with it.

Solution: Go back to basics and reteach Drop It (page 13). This can be a hard concept for some dogs to master, especially those that are easily excited by playing Fetch. But Rover should know how to drop an object, be it a leash or something more serious/dangerous.

★ BRING ME ★
A BAG OF LEAVES

- ⊙ **HAND SIGNAL**
- ✋ **VERBAL CUE:** "Get the bag"
- ⚙ **TOOLS:** Praise
- ⏱ **AVG. TIME:** 5-7 Days
- ✚ **DIFFICULTY:** Intermediate

Who doesn't need help with yard work? Whether you're hauling garbage bags full of leaves, dragging a tub filled with grass clippings or putting in new plants, have Rover do his share. Once he's mastered dragging the bag or tub, imagine the possibilities: Rover can learn to pull the hose off its stand (Name That Thingamajig, page 33; Tug It, page 23), fetch your garden gloves from across the yard (Name That Thingamajig, page 33; Fetch, page 31), even bring you the sprinkler for setup once the plants are in the ground (Name That Thingamajig, page 33; this trick)!

STEP-BY-STEP

1. Teach your dog the name of the bag (which should be closed with a tie) using Name That Thingamajig (page 33).

2. Show him the bag and say, "Tug, get the bag" (Tug It, page 23). Give him lots of praise.

Teach your dog the name of the bag (which should be closed with a tie) using Name That Thingamajig (page 33).

Show him the bag and say, "Tug, get the bag" (Tug It, page 23). Give him lots of praise.

2. Repeat again but step back a few feet back and tell him, "Tug, get the bag!" Once he begins moving toward you, even just one step, give him lots of praise.

3. Repeat and slowly work on building the distance that he brings the bag to you. If he drops the bag on his way to you, back up, shorten the distance and start again. Use the commands Tug and Get the Bag.

4. Practice three to five times a day for five to seven days.

 ADVICE FROM THE EXPERT

Dragging a bag of leaves or a tub isn't difficult once Rover knows how to Tug It (page 23). Start by teaching him the names of the bag and the tub. To make the trick easier, tie a big knot in the garbage bag so he has something to grab onto, and use a tub or bucket with a rope handle or soft rope attached.

PROBLEM SOLVING

Problem: Your little guy can't tug that big bag of leaves.

Solution: Make sure the weight of the bag is appropriate for your dog. It's best to start out with lighter bags to make it easier to drag, then move up to bigger bags as he learns.

Repeat and slowly work on building the distance that he brings the bag to you.

★ OPEN AND CATCH ★

Ever been to a minor league baseball game and watched a trick dog catch a flying Frisbee between innings? You can generate oohs and aahs by teaching Rover how to open his mouth and catch just about anything, from a tennis ball (page 43) to a Frisbee (page 44). This two-part trick is the foundational skill for any maneuver where you want to throw something and have your dog catch it in his mouth.

⊕ **HAND SIGNAL**
🐾 **VERBAL CUE:** "Open, Catch"
⚙ **TOOLS:** Praise and Treats
🕐 **AVG. TIME:** 5-7 Days
➕ **DIFFICULTY:** Intermediate

STEP-BY-STEP

1. Throw your dog's favorite treat gently towards him in a shallow trajectory. Tell him, "Open" as you toss it, then follow it with, "Catch." If he goes to retrieve the treat off the floor, allow it. Praise him.

2. Repeat three to five times each session. Make it short and fun! Practice for five to seven days.

🏅 **ADVICE FROM THE EXPERT**

You may have to coordinate the trajectory and the height of the treat as you toss it. Try to be as consistent as possible in the way you throw it.

🦴 **PROBLEM SOLVING**

Problem: Your dog keeps missing the treat, but then lunges to eat it off the floor.

Solution: Believe it or not, this isn't really a problem. Rover can learn pretty quickly that if he opens his mouth and catches the treat he'll get it that much more quickly.

CATCH A TENNIS BALL ★

Catching a tennis ball: It sounds simple and it is, once Rover has mastered Open and Catch (page 42). You can easily build on this trick. Impress your friends with Rover on the tennis court, catching balls as you gently serve them over the net! You can even softly hit him a grounder using a whiffle ball or gently bat him a shuttlecock.

⊕ **HAND SIGNAL**
ℬ **VERBAL CUE:** "Catch"
✿ **TOOLS:** Praise and Treats
🕐 **AVG. TIME:** 3-5 Days
✚ **DIFFICULTY:** Beginner

STEP-BY-STEP

1. Make sure he watches the ball, then tell him, "Open, catch" (page 42).

2. From there progress to tossing the ball towards him and saying, "Catch."

3. Practice several times a day for three to five days.

🎖 ADVICE FROM THE EXPERT

If your dog can't catch a ball right from the start, try bouncing the ball towards him until his skills improve. If your little guy can't get his mouth around a tennis ball you can always substitute a smaller rubber ball, but not something so small it could be a choking hazzard.

⦿ PROBLEM SOLVING

Problem: Your dog runs after the ball and retrieves it, but doesn't seem to grasp the concept of Catch.

Solution: Make sure Rover likes and is comfortable holding things in his mouth. Work on getting him used to holding it for short periods, all the while giving him lots and lots of praise.

★ CATCH A FRISBEE ★

You're ready for an NFL halftime show with this entertaining trick. If your dog is really talented at catching a flying disc, who knows? With practice he might even join Bling Bling, the 2012 mixed-breed winner of the Frisbee Dog World Championship!

Start teaching this trick very gently and from up close. This trick takes time, practice and patience. Rover may be able to fetch the Frisbee easily but it takes agility for him to catch the disc consistently, and for you to throw it consistently as well!

⊕ HAND SIGNAL
✋ VERBAL CUE: "Take it, Catch the Frisbee"
✿ TOOLS: Praise
◷ AVG. TIME: 7-10 Days
✚ DIFFICULTY: Advanced

STEP-BY-STEP

1. Practice a few Open and Catches (page 42) with a treat or a ball. Stand in front of your dog while he faces you in a stand. Before you toss the Frisbee, tease him with it a little bit. Get him interested in the disc. Shake it in front of him and tell him, "Take it" (sidebar, page 45). When he does, give him a treat and praise.

Tease your dog with the Frisbee to get him excited.

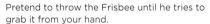

Pretend to throw the Frisbee until he tries to grab it from your hand.

Practice throwing the Frisbee the same way every time.

It will take some practice for your dog to catch the Frisbee consistently.

TAKE IT

Take It is one of those building-block commands that proves simple to teach and invaluable when progressing to tricks such as Catch a Frisbee and Carry the Present. Hold out a favorite toy towards Rover and say, "Take it." When he takes it, praise him. Practice a few times a day for a few days, and he should have it. Progress to an object in which he has little interest, such as a newspaper, saying, "Take it." When he takes it, offer lots of praise. If he won't take it, try training with a treat as a reward until he reliably responds.

🦴 PROBLEM SOLVING

Problem: You can't throw the Frisbee to your dog very well.

Solution: Practice! You need to learn how to throw the disc the right way and the same way every time. If you can't, hold off on trying to train Rover and perfect your own technique first.

2. Stand at an arm's length, and pretend to toss the Frisbee, but don't let go. Say, "Open, catch the Frisbee." Repeat a few more times. Once he starts grabbing the Frisbee while you are holding it, back up about 1 foot/0.3 m and toss it and say "Open, catch the Frisbee." Give him a treat and praise when he does.

3. Slowly back up and throw it from slightly further distances. Make certain you throw it in a low trajectory until he improves. When he gets the trick down, drop Open and simply say, "Catch the Frisbee." Eventually wean him off rewards.

4. Practice several times a day for seven to ten days.

★ BRING ME ★
THE NEWSPAPER

⊕ **HAND SIGNAL**

🅑 **VERBAL CUE:** "Get the paper"

⚙ **TOOLS:** Clicker, Praise and Treats

⏱ **AVG. TIME:** 5-7 Days

✚ **DIFFICULTY:** Intermediate

It's Sunday morning, there's snow on the ground, and the newspaper is lying in the driveway. No need to scamper out in your pajamas and slippers. Send Rover to do his business and fetch the paper at the same time!

Like many of the tricks in this chapter, Bring Me the Newspaper builds on the concepts of identifying an object (Name That Thingamajig, page 33), retrieving that object (Fetch, page 31), and dropping it at your command (Drop It, page 13). If your dog has mastered these commands for other objects then this should come together very quickly.

STEP-BY-STEP

1. Take a lightweight weekly paper and wrap it tightly with masking tape. Teach your dog the name "newspaper" using the instructions for Name That Thingamajig (page 33).

Teach your dog the name "newspaper" using the instructions for Name That Thingamajig (page 33).

2. Throw it out a few feet for Rover and tell him, "Get the paper." Once he picks it up you can click but no treat.

3. Call him to "Come" (page 12) and click again. Throw the newspaper and say, "Get the paper, fetch" (Fetch, page 31). Click away, give him tons of praise and give him a treat or two.

4. Repeat this training sequence, each time throwing the taped paper a little further away.

5. Once he starts coming back to you automatically, you can drop the "Come" and "Fetch" commands and just use "Get the paper."

6. Advance by adding in, "Drop it" (page 13) and using a real newspaper, without masking tape.

7. Practice three to five times a day for five to seven days.

Throw it out a few feet for Rover and tell him, "Get the paper." Once he picks it up you can click but no treat.

 ADVICE FROM THE EXPERT

There are two keys to success with training this trick: Your dog should love retrieving, and he should be very comfortable holding things in his mouth.

PROBLEM SOLVING

Problem: Your dog fetches the paper but refuses to bring it to you.

Solution: Walk away, ignore him and wait him out. Eventually he will come over to you looking for praise.

Advance by adding in, "Drop it" (page 13) and using a real newspaper, without masking tape.

★ GET THE MAIL ★

Here's one of the most impressive tricks in this book: teaching your dog to get the mail. Imagine how impressed your neighbors—even your mail carrier—will be when Rover trots casually down the driveway, puts his paws up on the mailbox, opens the door with a quick tug, pulls out the letters, noses the door shut and trots back to your side!

➕ **HAND SIGNAL**
✌ **VERBAL CUE:** "Get the mail"
⚙ **TOOLS:** Praise and Treats
🕐 **AVG. TIME:** 7-10 Days
➕ **DIFFICULTY:** Advanced

STEP-BY-STEP

1. Start with a large, thick envelope and a mailbox that your dog can reach. Show him the mail and teach him the word "mail" using Name That Thingamajig (page 33).

2. Let him see you place the mail in the mailbox and close the door.

3. Tie a soft rope or bandana on the mailbox door. Show it to him and tell him, "Tug it." Repeat several times a day and reward him with a treat and praise. Don't move to the next step until he's reliably opening the mailbox door.

Show him the mail before you close the mailbox door.

Point to the rope on the mailbox and say, "Tug it."

Rover will open the door with a quick tug ...

4. Move on to "Tug, get the mail." The goal is have him pull the door open, pull the mail out of the box and bring it to you. Repeat several times a day until he's got this sequence of commands down, then transition to using "get the mail" alone. As he completes each task and moves to the next be sure to click, reward and give him lots of praise.

5. Repeat this two to three times each day and it should be reliable in seven to ten days.

6. For the advanced version, add Bump (page 27) to teach Rover to go back and close the mailbox door and even push the flag down once he's delivered the mail to you.

ADVICE FROM THE EXPERT

Train your dog using a mailbox he can reach. If you have a short dog like a corgi, you can use a low mailbox (about the height of a table or ottoman) but add in steps for Paws Up (sidebar page 19). If your dog can reach the box, simply skip the Paws Up command.

PROBLEM SOLVING

Problem: Using a life-size mailbox and stringing together all those tasks is too complex.

Solution: Use a trick-size version of the mailbox, break the trick down into parts and teach your dog to complete one task at a time or just one task alone. Any trick that involves human actions is entertaining!

... and grab the mail inside. Success!

CARRY THE PRESENT

★ **HAND SIGNAL**

ᛒ **VERBAL CUE:** "Carry the present, Go to _____"

⚙ **TOOLS:** Praise

🕐 **AVG. TIME:** 5-7 Days

✚ **DIFFICULTY:** Intermediate

I love this trick! Years ago I helped a friend train his Yorkshire terrier to carry the box containing the engagement ring over to his intended bride. You can imagine the oohs and aahs the woman received when she told the story! And here's part two: The dog followed up with a bouquet of flowers. What a way to wow her!

Start with a small plain box and move to a wrapped gift or small gift bag. You'll also need a second person whom your dog knows by name.

STEP-BY-STEP

1. Give the small box to your dog and say, "Take it" (sidebar, page 45). Then tell him, "Go to Auntie."

2. Have Auntie call your dog, "Come, come" (page 12). As soon as your dog gets to Auntie have her give him lots of praise.

3. Repeat this several times, then say "Go to Auntie, carry the present." Over time transition to the "Carry the present" command alone.

4. Practice several times a day for five to seven days.

 ADVICE FROM THE EXPERT

It may sound obvious, but this isn't a great trick for bulldogs, who drool a lot, or for any dog who produces lots of saliva.

PROBLEM SOLVING

Problem: Your dog takes the present, but wants to play with it or chew on it.

Solution: Get your dog used to handling the box gently. Correct him if he starts chewing on it or tearing it up.

CHAPTER THREE

DO YOUR THING

Here's a collection of tricks that's sure to bring on a round of applause, whether Rover performs each trick individually or you teach him to complete a string of commands, one right after another.

Once your dog has a series of tricks in place, such as Nod Yes (page 54), Wag Your Tail (page 63) and Kiss (page 64), you can make up an entire conversation or a multi-part joke to entertain your friends. Imagine the following scenario: You ask Rover if he loves you; he nods yes. You ask Rover if he'll make a pact to elope; he wags his tail. You tell Rover, "Let's seal it with a kiss." He kisses your cheek.

Imagine telling the various lines of a joke one at a time and cueing Rover to Nod Yes (page 54), Shake Your Head No (page 55), Head Down (page 52), Walk Backwards (page 67) and so on at the appropriate times. This is great entertainment that even your kids can learn to do with your dog. Who knows, maybe Rover will one day become the star of the annual neighborhood talent show!

★ HEAD UP ★ AND HEAD DOWN

Teaching Rover to mimic any kind of human action is always a great way to elicit a laugh or two. Head Up is a great place to start. Once your dog will put his head down on command you as well, can add a funny intro phrase, such as "Who stole the cookies from the cookie jar?" or link the words "Are you a dog food snob?" to the head lift.

⊙ HAND SIGNAL
🖰 VERBAL CUE: "Head up, Head down"
⚙ TOOLS: Clicker, Praise and Treats
🕐 AVG. TIME: 3-5 Days
✚ DIFFICULTY: Beginner

STEP-BY-STEP

1. Place your dog in the Down position (page 14). Push down gently on his head and say, "Head down, good dog." Don't give the treat.

2. If he brings his head up say, "Head up," then click and treat. Do it again.

3. Repeat five to ten times the first session. Make sure you're not clicking and treating the down, as the click will rev him up. You want him nice and relaxed for the head down.

4. Repeat three to five times for several days.

🏅 ADVICE FROM THE EXPERT

It will be hard to teach Head Down to a revved up dog. He needs to be relaxed in order to really grasp the Head Down command. Use a calm voice and slow and gentle motions to help relax Rover as you teach this.

These two commands can be taught simultaneously, but be sure to use your clicker along with a treat to fine-tune your timing on the reward.

🦴 PROBLEM SOLVING

Problem: Your dog pops up, out of his down position, when you say, "Head up."

Solution: Try refining your timing for the click. The more exact you can be, the sooner he'll make the connection between what he's doing and what you want.

★ GO TO YOUR PLACE ★

⊕ HAND SIGNAL
🔖 VERBAL CUE: "Go to your place"
✿ TOOLS: Praise and Treats
🕐 AVG. TIME: 7-10 Days
✛ DIFFICULTY: Intermediate

Here's a trick that's both practical and fun. The practical application is simple: You're in the kitchen making dinner and you want Rover out from underfoot. Simply send him to his place and voilà! You can cook undisturbed. For an entertaining version of this trick, link the command to a funny phrase such as "Where's your favorite place to sleep?" or "Where's your happy place?"

STEP-BY-STEP

1. Find a spot for your dog such as a bed or a crate. You can have several spots, but teach them one at a time.

2. Place your dog between you and where you want him to go. Tell him, "Go to your place" as you continually move in towards him. If he veers off course, cut him off. Think of shepherds herding sheep. Keep him between you and where you want him to go.

3. When he gets very close to the place, throw the treat down at the place and let him chase it. Give him lots and lots of praise. Repeat this three times the first session.

4. Repeat five to ten times over a week. Once you've taught the word "place" you can teach him, "Go to your bed," "Go to your crate" and so on.

 ADVICE FROM THE EXPERT

This is a great way to relax a hyper dog. Sending him to his place can take the edge off. You can start with a crate and transition if needed, but any spot should work if correctly taught.

🦴 PROBLEM SOLVING

Problem: Rover's in his place but he doesn't want to stay put.

Solution: If he moves, march him back to the spot and make him stay there using Stay (page 11). Stay close by watching him for a minute, then build up to five minutes, then ten, and so on. Over time advance his "stay time" to thirty minutes. This is enough time for the dog to truly relax.

Problem: He'll stay in his place but gets up as soon as you leave the room.

Solution: Again, practice makes perfect. Repeat the training method outlined above but start moving around the room or the house when he's in his place. Correct him if he moves. Eventually Rover should go to his place, lie down and stay there until you release him.

★ NOD YES ★

- ⊕ **HAND SIGNAL**
- ℬ **VERBAL CUE:** "Nod yes"
- ⚙ **TOOLS:** Clicker and Treats
- ◷ **AVG. TIME:** 5-7 Days
- ✚ **DIFFICULTY:** Beginner

A trick like Nod Yes can be customized to elicit laughs, and the same goes for tricks like Shake Your Head No (page 55) and Bark to Go Out (page 60). Once he's got the nodding head movement in place, link it to a funny phrase of your choosing such as "Are you the most amazing dog in town?" or "Am I the best dog trainer you know?"

STEP-BY-STEP

1. Place your dog into Sit-Stay (page 10) and hold a treat.

2. Make certain your dog sees the treat, then bring the treat up and down. Your dog's head should move up and down in a nod as he watches the treat. Click and treat.

3. Practice five times using the command "Nod yes" and the clicker.

4. Repeat two to three times a day for five to seven days.

🏅 ADVICE FROM THE EXPERT

Using proper body language and creating a bond with your dog are key here. Make sure you are laser-focused on your dog and that he's watching your every move. Work in an area without distractions for the best results.

🦴 PROBLEM SOLVING

Problem: Your dog is too focused on the treat to catch the subtleties of this trick.

Solution: Teaching him Nod Yes or Shake Your Head No (page 55) takes a lot of focus, and if his focus is only on the treat then you've got to break that connection. Calm your body language and use a quiet tone of voice. Be very patient and try teaching only with praise and/or the clicker.

★ SHAKE YOUR HEAD NO ★

Looking for quick and easy dinner party entertainment? One of the funniest ways to use Shake Your Head No, as with Nod Yes (previous trick), is to link your dog's headshake to a funny question or current event. Here are a few examples: "Rover, do you like rap music?" or "Is the Democratic party going win the election?"

⊕ HAND SIGNAL
🖰 VERBAL CUE: "Shake no"
✿ TOOLS: Clicker and Treats
🕐 AVG. TIME: 5-7 Days
✚ DIFFICULTY: Beginner

STEP-BY-STEP

1. Blow in your dog's ear and say, "Shake no." The blow in the ear will get your dog to shake his head. As soon as he does, click and treat.

2. Repeat two to three times a day for five to seven days.

🎗 ADVICE FROM THE EXPERT

This is a trick that requires you to capture your dog's action, so be ready with your clicker when you blow in his ear.

🦴 PROBLEM SOLVING

Problem: Your dog is too excited to catch the subtleties of this trick.

Solution: Calm him down and help him focus. Use whatever relaxation techniques work best for you and your dog: calm voice, quiet body language, no distractions, etc. If it's not working, back off and try the training on a different day or at a different time of day.

★ CROSS YOUR LEGS ★

Certain breeds, such as Italian greyhounds and certain terriers, will cross their legs naturally. Teach this polite and refined trick to a bigger dog and it's a move that looks really cute! Once Rover has the trick down pat, link the trick to your favorite lead-in, such as, "Emily Post is coming for dinner!"

⊕ **HAND SIGNAL**

ℬ **VERBAL CUE:** "Cross Your Legs"

✿ **TOOLS:** Clicker and Treats

🕑 **AVG. TIME:** 3-5 Days

✚ **DIFFICULTY:** Beginner

STEP-BY-STEP

1. Put your dog in the Down position (page 14). Place your clicker in your left hand and treats in your right hand. Let him focus on the hand with the treats.

2. Touch his leg with your right hand and let him watch you move it over to your left, with the goal of getting him to move his left leg over his right leg. Tell him, "Cross your legs" then click and treat.

3. Repeat this six to eight times then switch to the left hand, moving your left hand to your right with the goal of causing your dog's right foot to cross over his left.

4. Practice three to five times a day for three to five days. Make sure he's mastered one paw before you move to the next.

🏅 **ADVICE FROM THE EXPERT**

Watch to see what your dog naturally does. Some dogs favor one leg crossing over the other.

🦴 **PROBLEM SOLVING**

Problem: Rover already crosses his legs.

Solution: This isn't a problem! This is an action you can capture using the clicker, then associate with the verbal cue and reward.

★ WIPE YOUR FEET ★

Imagine a dog so polite he stops to wipe his feet at the door just like a proper gentleman! That's your dog once you teach this cute and practical trick through regular routine. Before long you can teach him to stop and wipe his feet before he jumps into your car or after a walk in the woods.

⊕ HAND SIGNAL
✋ VERBAL CUE: "Wipe your feet"
✿ TOOLS: Praise and Treats
⏱ AVG. TIME: 2-3 Days
➕ DIFFICULTY: Intermediate

STEP-BY-STEP

1. Place your dog in a Stand-Stay (Stay, step 9, page 11) and put a towel on the floor.

2. Tell your dog, "Left paw, touch it" (Touch it, page 22), then lift the left paw and wipe it on the towel. Repeat several times, rewarding with a treat.

3. When the dog performs reliably, add, "Wipe your feet," saying, "Left paw, touch it, wipe your feet." Reward any movement of his paw on the towel. Repeat a few times a day for two to three days.

4. Once he's reliably performing, drop the Touch It command.

5. Repeat steps one through four with the right paw.

6. Tell your dog, "Left paw, wipe your feet, right paw, wipe your feet." You may need to lift the dog's paws the first few times so he understands you want him to move both at once. Reward and praise. Repeat a few times a day for two to three days.

7. Once the dog wipes both paws several times, drop the left and right references and use, "Wipe Your Feet." Practice two to three times a day for two to three days.

🏅 ADVICE FROM THE EXPERT

Using the Touch It command (page 22) to teach this trick is the easiest method. If you want your dog to wipe one particular paw for a specific scenario, simply stop at "left paw, wipe your feet" or "right paw, wipe your feet."

★ ROLL OVER ★

This is a fun and entertaining trick that isn't that difficult to teach. Imagine your dog rolling on his back in the grass, happy and smiling, then rolling over and popping up on command! I like to combine this trick with a few other "happy" tricks for a fun skit. These include Wag Your Tail (page 63), Shake Your Body (page 59) and Chase Your Tail (page 130).

HAND SIGNAL
VERBAL CUE: "Roll over"
TOOLS: Treats
AVG. TIME: 5-7 Days
DIFFICULTY: Intermediate

STEP-BY-STEP

1. Put your dog in the Down position (page 14).

2. Kneel in front of him holding a treat. Move the treat in the direction you want him to roll and say, "Roll over" in a very calm voice. Give him the treat for any rolling motion.

3. Repeat five to ten times the first session, then advance to luring him onto his back and over to the other side. As he comes out of the roll, use a happy voice to praise him.

4. Repeat several times a day and within a week Rover should have this down pat.

ADVICE FROM THE EXPERT

Although I call this a happy trick, you'll want to use a calm, relaxed voice and quiet body language when teaching the first part of this trick. It may seem coun-terintuitive, but you need a dog to be relaxed to get him to lie down and go onto his back. Once he's on his back, use a happy voice as he rolls over. At this point in the trick he's transitioned from relaxed to energetic!

Keep in mind that a dog feels very vulnerable on his back. This is the most submissive position he knows. You'll need a strong bond and lots of trust for him to perform this trick, but it's doable for any dog!

PROBLEM SOLVING

Problem: Your dog hasn't learned to relax enough to go over to his side and/or his back.

Solution: I refer to this as a tense Down-Stay (page 14), where Rover is sitting in a Sphinx-like position with hips and legs flat and straight, his rather than a Down with his hindquarters splayed to the side. You'll need to back up and review Down (page 14) as well as the Dead Dog (page 17) in order to ensure he will relax on command.

★ SHAKE YOUR BODY ★

⊕ HAND SIGNAL

🔊 VERBAL CUE: "Shake your body"

⚙ TOOLS: Clicker and Treats

⏱ AVG. TIME: 5-7 Days

✚ DIFFICULTY: Beginner

If you love dogs then you know what to expect right after your dog comes out of the bath: a big body shake that sprays water everywhere! If you remove the water but keep the shake, you've got a trick that's sure to entertain your friends. Like a few of the other tricks in this book, you need to capture the action in order to train this. After all, shaking the body is really just a natural movement for most dogs.

STEP-BY-STEP

1. Each time your dog is in the tub, or as soon as he gets out of the tub, he will shake his body.

2. Tell him, "Shake your body," then click and treat. You want to capture the action.

3. You can also do this while you are drying your dog. If you rub him vigorously and get him excited he will also stop to shake his body. Say, "Shake your body."

4. Practice three to five times a day for five to seven days.

🏅 ADVICE FROM THE EXPERT

As with all "captured action" tricks you've got to carry your clicker and treat with you to the bathing area. Unlike some captured action tricks, however, it's much easier to anticipate exactly when this will happen, meaning it's that much easier to reward!

Any time you're teaching a captured action trick keep these tips in mind: Have your clicker ready, pay close attention to your dog and try to anticipate what your dog is going to do.

🦴 PROBLEM SOLVING

Problem: Your dog is excited as he comes out of the bathtub and isn't making the connection with the clicker.

Solution: No surprise here—training any trick requires focus, and if your dog is only thinking about getting away from the tub this may not be the right time for training! Instead, try to capture your dog shaking his body at another time, such as first thing in the morning. Have your clicker ready!

BARK TO GO OUT ★

⊕ HAND SIGNAL

🐾 VERBAL CUE: "Want to go out?"

✿ TOOLS: Praise, Clicker and Treats

⏱ AVG. TIME: 5-7 Days

✛ DIFFICULTY: Beginner

All dogs communicate, whether they prefer barking, whining, playful growling, all of the above or even something else! That means once you've taught your dog how to Speak (page 16) it's easy to teach your dog how to use that bark to communicate important things, such as when he needs to go out. Once he's nailed this simple trick you can have him bark the answers to all kinds of funny questions, even simple math problems (Do Your Arithmetic, page 119)!

STEP-BY-STEP

1. Anticipate when your dog needs to go out. Some dogs stand by the door, others whine, others actually paw at the door. When you see this, grab a treat and use two commands together: Speak (page 16) and Want to Go Out?

Hold a treat in your hand and say, "Speak" and "Want to go out?
....

🏅 ADVICE FROM THE EXPERT

If you find your dog responds better to the clicker than a treat feel free to use the clicker here. The key is to capture the exact action you want (one bark, not two) at exactly the right moment.

🦴 PROBLEM SOLVING

Problem: Your dog won't stop barking

Solution: Rover should know the meaning of the word "no" by now. When he barks, tell him, "No." If that doesn't work, tell him, "No" and give him a small tug on the leash. If that's not effective, use a squirt bottle of water and tell him, "No bark." (FYI, don't use a squirt bottle with a breed like a Labrador. This will increase the barking because he will love getting wet!) Spray with a stream, not a mist, and aim directly at his face. Don't worry, it won't hurt him, just annoy him, and teach him not to bark.

Open the door for your dog.

Encourage him to go out the door.

Give him the treat and praise when he comes back in.

2. Once he responds, even if it's just a wag of the tail, click, open the door and encourage him to go out. Give him the treat and praise when he comes back in. Repeat this process several times.

3. If the dog responds reliably giving his out signal, but won't bark, review the Speak command (page 16) several times.

4. After reviewing Speak, continue practicing step one, saying, "Speak, want to go out," but only click/treat if the dog barks once (you don't want him barking multiple times every time he needs to go out).

5. Once the dog regularly barks when he needs to go out, drop Speak and repeat, "Want to go out" several times.

6. Practice several times a day for five to seven days.

★ SHAKE YOUR PAW ★

● **HAND SIGNAL**
🐾 **VERBAL CUE:** "Shake your paw"
⚙ **TOOLS:** Treats
🕐 **AVG. TIME:** 3-5 Days
✚ **DIFFICULTY:** Beginner

Chances are pretty high that your dog already knows this action. Pawing at something comes naturally to most dogs, and translating that into holding his paw up, near your hand, is pretty simple. The fun comes when you change up the command: Try making up your own verbal command, such as, "Give me a low five" or even, "Give me a fist pump."

STEP-BY-STEP

1. Place your dog in a Sit-Stay (Stay, step 8, page 11) in front of you. Hold the treat in your hand but don't let him see it.

2. Give your dog the opportunity to sniff or paw at your hand. If he doesn't sniff or paw at your hand, lift up his paw, tell him, "Shake your paw," then give him the treat.

3. Repeat at least five to ten times the first session, then two to three times a day for three to five days.

 ADVICE FROM THE EXPERT

This may be the fastest trick to teach. Before you even begin, try offering your hand to your dog. Sometimes this alone is enough!

PROBLEM SOLVING

Problem: Your dog paws at the treat but won't hold his paw up steadily in the air.

Solution: It's important that the treat be used as a reward, not a lure. Don't let him actually see the treat until he does the trick, otherwise he may become distracted by the treat and lose focus on what you're saying.

WAG YOUR TAIL

HAND SIGNAL

✍ **VERBAL CUE:** "Wag your tail"

⚙ **TOOLS:** Clicker and Treats

🕐 **AVG. TIME:** 5-7 Days

✛ **DIFFICULTY:** Beginner

Tail wagging is the number one visual cue that your dog is friendly, happy and/or excited. And because it's something that dogs do naturally, teaching your dog to wag his tail on command makes a great trick! Once Rover has it mastered just imagine the funny yes/no questions you can use with a tail wag as the yes: Do you like chocolate ice cream? Are dogs superior to cats? Will the Boston Red Sox beat the New York Yankees next weekend?

STEP-BY-STEP

1. Learn what excites your dog and when he starts wagging, tell him, "Wag your tail." Click and treat.

2. Repeat again five to ten times the first session.

3. Repeat several times a day for five to seven days.

🏅 ADVICE FROM THE EXPERT

Like so many natural actions this is one you have to capture, but it should be fairly easy if you know what excites your dog. Have your clicker ready, pay close attention to your dog and try to anticipate the exact second he'll start wagging his tail.

🦴 PROBLEM SOLVING

Problem: Your dog wags his tail, but not very enthusiastically.

Solution: Express more excitement with your tone and body language. There's no need to tamp down your own enthusiasm when teaching this trick!

★ KISS ★

Gimme a kiss! Give me some sugar! What dog owner doesn't love getting a smooch from his or her favorite pooch? If your dog doesn't already do this on his own, no worries. This is one of the easiest tricks to teach. If he does do it on his own, just keep praising him—no reason to add the food motivator.

⊕ **HAND SIGNAL**
🕭 **VERBAL CUE:** "Kiss me"
✿ **TOOLS:** Treats
🕐 **AVG. TIME:** 3-5 Days
✚ **DIFFICULTY:** Beginner

STEP-BY-STEP

1. Put a tiny smear of cream cheese, peanut butter or cheese sauce or your cheek.

2. Tell your dog, "Kiss me." The reward is whatever they are licking off of your cheek.

3. Repeat this five to ten times each session for three to five days, then move on to saying "Kiss me" without the reward.

 ADVICE FROM THE EXPERT

Want to step this up? Hold a tiny treat between your teeth and teach Rover to grab it. Eventually you can put the treat elsewhere (e.g., on your head) and prompt him with a funny question such as, "Have you seen my glasses?"

🦴 **PROBLEM SOLVING**

Problem: Your dog is only motivated by food.

Solution: Teach this trick without the incentive, but really lay on the praise when he's successful. This is true of any trick you're trying to teach a dog who's primarily focused on food. You need to transition him away from the rewards for his tummy and towards the simple reward of your praise. Tap into his desire to please you instead of relying on his interest in food.

★ LIFT YOUR LEG ★

If your dog is male then you already know what happens when you take him for a walk: He stops to lift his leg at least fifty times! This trick replicates that action but without Rover relieving himself. Your guests won't know that, though, so this trick can be used to play a practical joke on someone!

⊕ **HAND SIGNAL**

✋ **VERBAL CUE:** "Lift your leg"

✿ **TOOLS:** Praise

🕐 **AVG. TIME:** 5-7 Days

✚ **DIFFICULTY:** Beginner

STEP-BY-STEP

1. Place your dog in a Stand-Stay (Stay, step 9, page 11).

2. Reach down behind his knee and lightly tickle him between his leg and stomach. Tell him, "Lift your leg, lift your leg."

3. Do this for short periods of time, fifteen to forty-five seconds the first time.

4. After five to ten times in a row of the dog starting to lift his leg when you tickle, start moving your hand back and scratch the root of his tail, saying, "Lift your leg." Practice until the dog reliably lifts his leg with the command and the tail scratch.

5. After the dog reliably performs with the command and the tail scratch, remove the tail scratch and practice with no touch, saying, "Lift your leg."

6. Practice three to five times a day for five to seven days.

🏅 ADVICE FROM THE EXPERT

This is a natural movement for male dogs, but not necessarily for female pooches. Be patient as you teach females this move.

🦴 PROBLEM SOLVING

Problem: Your dog doesn't get it.

Solution: Although I like to teach this trick using praise and a tickling movement, it can also be taught using a treat and/or clicker. You can also show the dog what you want him to do by physically picking up his leg while you say, "Lift your leg."

WIPE YOUR MOUTH

HAND SIGNAL

VERBAL CUE: "Wipe your mouth"

TOOLS: Clicker and Treats

AVG. TIME: 5-7 Days

DIFFICULTY: Beginner

If you've got kids, you know how many times you've told them to wipe their mouth, and not with their sleeve or shirt! Here's a trick that every polite dog should know. This is especially funny if you string it together with a few other "good manners" tricks, such as Cross Your Legs (page 56) and Wipe Your Feet (page 57). You can teach Rover the prompt to a string of tricks using an intro phrase such as, "Miss Manners is coming!"

STEP-BY-STEP

1. Put a small piece of masking tape on the side of your dog's muzzle.

2. Rover will scratch at the tape. Say, "Wipe your mouth," click and give him a treat. Keep in mind this is a "captured action" trick. Repeat this three to five times the first session.

3. Repeat several times a day for five to seven days.

ADVICE FROM THE EXPERT

You know the routine with captured action training: Keep the clicker in your hand, be vigilant and lay on the praise when he gets it right.

PROBLEM SOLVING

Problem: The masking tape approach isn't working.

Solution: Rub a tiny bit of peanut butter on his muzzle. He'll paw at it—be sure to capture the action with a click—then likely lick his paws for ten minutes. Once he's mastered Wipe Your Mouth, you can also turn Lick Your Paws into another on-command trick by capturing the action and clicking.

WALK BACKWARDS/ BACK UP

⊕ **HAND SIGNAL**

Ｂ **VERBAL CUE:** "Back up"

✿ **TOOLS:** Praise

🕐 **AVG. TIME:** 5-7 Days

✛ **DIFFICULTY:** Beginner

What could be funnier than your dog walking backwards, just like Michael Jackson performing his famous moonwalk? Pair this with your favorite Michael Jackson song and the laughs are sure to follow! Once he's mastered this move, create your own musical scenario or on-command sequence by stringing together Walk Backwards with tricks such as Head Up and Head Down (page 52) or Walk on Front Legs (page 72). You can also use Walk Backwards as a transition between other tricks.

STEP-BY-STEP

1. Start with your dog standing in front of you. Walk towards him saying, "Back up, back up."

2. Once he backs up, move forward five or six paces. Give him lots of praise.

3. Repeat five to ten times the first session, then repeat several times a day for a week.

🎖 **ADVICE FROM THE EXPERT**

Be patient when teaching this trick. Walking backwards isn't a movement that comes naturally to dogs. Take your time and use lots of praise.

🦴 **PROBLEM SOLVING**

Problem: Your dog doesn't walk backwards but instead turns around and tries to run away.

Solution: Use your leg to block him. Bring your leg straight up in front of him to prevent him from turning. If that doesn't work, try teaching this trick in a long, narrow hallway where your dog can't turn around. This way he has no place to go but backwards. Add your leg as a secondary tool if needed.

DIG ON COMMAND ★

● **HAND SIGNAL**
♫ **VERBAL CUE:** "Dig"
✿ **TOOLS:** Clicker, Praise and Treats
⏱ **AVG. TIME:** 5-7 Days
✚ **DIFFICULTY:** Beginner

Everyone knows a dog that loves to dig, whether it's a breed that's naturally wired to get his paws dirty, such as a rat terrier, or a pooch who just loves to dig the way some of us love to garden! Just like any behavior that dogs do naturally, turning the action into an on-command trick is always good for a few laughs! Be sure to teach your dog to dig in the right place, and have a good solid "no" in your back pocket for spontaneous diggers!

STEP-BY-STEP

1. Show your dog one or two treats. When he takes them, give him a click and reward him with the treats. Repeat three times.

2. Take the treat and throw a little bit of dirt on top. Let him dig to get it while telling him, "Dig," pointing at the dirt and clicking at the same time. Keep encouraging with "Dig" and rewarding as he digs.

Bury a treat in the dirt.

Use the command "Dig" and point to the dirt.

3. Bury a ball or favorite toy in the dirt, putting one or two treats with it if he needs the scent to encourage him. Use the Dig command. Lay on the praise when he finds it.

4. Eventually he'll dig on command without the treats, but be sure to praise each success.

5. Practice three to five times a day for five to seven days.

Move to burying a ball in the dirt.

🏵 ADVICE FROM THE EXPERT

Make sure your dog is digging for and touching the toy with his paws, not just his nose. Dogs will be inclined to use their noses, especially since they're looking for the scent of the toy and/or treat. If the dog is using his nose, go back to basics and reinforce the Touch It command (page 22).

🦴 PROBLEM SOLVING

Problem: Your dog isn't really inclined to dig and/or he's not particularly interested in the treat.

Solution: Use a treat that really drives him crazy, such as sliced hot dogs or even a tiny crumble of cooked hamburger. Don't use too much, just tiny piece or two to pique his interest, and eventually use the special treat alongside a regular treat to wean him off the people food.

Use the Dig command to encourage him to find the ball.

★ SCRATCH YOURSELF ★

Imagine Rover scratching himself with his hind legs, first his right and then his left. What a dance move, and one that's guaranteed to elicit giggles. Keep in mind that some dogs will want to sit down and scratch themselves. This can be funny too, but the ultimate goal here is to have him stand on three legs. The altered posture is what makes the move look funny!

STEP-BY-STEP

1. Get on the floor with your dog and find his tickle spots. You'll know when you have found when he starts moving his leg uncontrollably. Once he does, tell him, "Scratch, scratch." Click and treat.

2. Once you've done this several times, place him in a Sit-Stay (Stay, step 8, page 11) and scratch his breastbone area. This should produce a conditioned reflex and once it does, he will start scratching himself. Tell him, "Scratch, scratch" then click and treat.

3. Practice several times a day for five to seven days. For an advanced version, teach him to scratch himself while standing.

🏅 ADVICE FROM THE EXPERT

The key here is finding the tickle spot, usually located on his belly right below his rib cage, in front of his hind-quarters. You may need to experiment a bit before you find the exact spot that brings on that spontaneous movement. Be patient.

🦴 PROBLEM SOLVING

Problem: Rover's not responding consistently to the tickling.

Solution: Sometimes all you need is a light touch, using just your fingertips. Move slowly and don't use a strong, open hand. The goal is to be very precise with a soft movement.

★ CHAPTER FOUR ★

CIRCUS TRICKS

Who doesn't love the circus? The smell of popcorn, the excitement of the big top, the jumping and rolling clowns, the trapeze artists flying overhead—and let's not forget the dancing, prancing and performing dogs! This chapter will teach you a full assortment of fun and entertaining tricks designed to showcase your dog's center ring abilities. I guarantee you won't need a special costume or props to elicit plenty of applause.

If you and your kids want to put on your own circus with Rover and a few trained neighborhood dog friends, this chapter will give you a full playbook for planning your own entertaining performance. Just having Rover Walk on Front Legs (page 72), Push a Carriage (page 82) and master the Teeter-totter (page 92) is impressive. When you add in slightly more advanced tricks such as the Shell Game (page 100) or Weave Cones (page 90), Rover is sure to amaze your gathering.

Don't forget the basic tenets for trick-training: You're the boss, and don't forget to have fun. Now let's join the circus!

WALK ON FRONT LEGS ★

Think back to the last time you went to the circus. Remember the band of tumbling, joshing and laughing clowns? I'll bet there was one in the group that could walk on his hands, right? If anyone says your dog can't clown around in the same way, they're wrong. All dogs, and especially toy and/or smaller breeds, can learn this funny balancing trick!

Learning how to do a handstand or a cartwheel takes time and practice. So will teaching Rover to first stand on, and then walk on his front legs. Achieving the correct positioning for solid and steady balance is critical, as is plenty of patience.

STEP-BY-STEP

1. Sit on your knees. With your dog in a standing position, gently lift up his hindquarters. Lift slowly, but not straight up, into a wheelbarrow position. Work slowly and gently so your dog can feel his center of gravity change.

2. Let your dog get comfortable with going upside down, into the wheelbarrow position. Tuck his hindquarters in tightly by holding them with your hand and resting them on your knees. If your dog is short, have him stand his back legs on your knees, rather then tucking them in. Hold him on your knees as he learns to balance for longer periods. This takes time and practice.

Help Rover get used to being upside down.

Rest his hind feet on your knees for teaching balance.

Spot your dog while he builds the muscle strength needed to hold the position.

3. Once he is comfortable you'll feel a difference in how he's steadying himself on you. You can move to just holding him up while you sit on your knees.

4. Eventually he won't need as much help. You can start letting go of him for small amounts of time, building up to longer and longer periods. Continue to spot him with your hands as his muscle strength grows.

5. Once he's comfortable standing on his front legs on his own you can slowly, gently nudge him forward and use the command "walk." Don't force it too quickly. Let him show you how comfortable he is and how fast he can go. One step forward is progress! Say "walk" and give him lots and lots of praise.

6. As he practices stepping forward, continue spotting him with your hand behind him, but don't let him lean on you.

7. Give him praise after one step. The next time make him take two steps, and so on.

8. Practice daily until he can walk on his own.

Continue spotting him while he learns to step forward.

 ADVICE FROM THE EXPERT

Your dog needs two things to be successful at this trick. First, he must build up the strength to hold the position. He also needs to get used to being upside down. This is not a comfortable position for a dog, so be very patient when teaching this move.

PROBLEM SOLVING

Problem: Rover holds the position but can't walk forward.

Solution: Assuming you've practiced this move enough for him to build up muscle strength, try positioning him on your knees and gently moving your knees forward. Spot him so he doesn't fall out of balance. Nudge him forward very slowly. Nudging him forward too quickly will definitely work against you.

★ UPWARD DOG AND ★ DOWNWARD DOG

● **HAND SIGNAL**
🖐 **VERBAL CUE:** "Up dog, Down dog"
⚙ **TOOLS:** Praise and Treats
🕐 **AVG. TIME:** 5-7 Days
＋ **DIFFICULTY:** Beginner

This pair of tricks comes right from the yoga mat. Just imagine how much fun you can have combining these moves with a few props—yoga mat, yoga block, a headband for your pooch—and a few other tricks, such as Turn the Lights Off (page 111) and Close Your Eyes (page 84). You can also teach your dog to bring you the rolled-up yoga mat or block with Name That Thingamajig (page 33).

Ready to take it even further? Create an entire sports-related show using these tricks as the warm-up or cooldown and Play Golf (page 140), Play Basketball (page 136) or Play Baseball (page 134) in between!

STEP-BY-STEP

1. Have Rover standing. Place your left arm under his belly and a small treat in your right hand in front of his nose.

2. Slowly move the treat along his muzzle and down his chest, almost like you are outlining his body. Once you get to his front legs, run the treat between his front legs and towards his front paws and the floor. Don't give him the treat, just let him follow the lure.

It is easiest to teach Upward Dog and Downward Dog at the same time, but I recommend teaching Downward Dog first, as this is the more natural of the two movements.

PROBLEM SOLVING

Problem: Rover's too focused on the treat to grasp what you're teaching.

Solution: Interrupt that amped-up energy. Break away from training and heel him (sidebar, page 12) for 10 or 15 feet/ 3 to 4.6 m, then try again.

Problem: Your dog is very excited and can't focus.

Solution: Both of these movements come naturally to a dog. Stop and consider when they happen: Just after Rover's gotten up from a nap and he's stretching himself awake. Successfully teaching the tricks, then, means Rover's got to be relaxed. Never be afraid, with this trick or others, to put away the treats and leave the training for another day if your dog isn't in the right frame of mind.

3. Use your left arm under his belly to gently force Rover to bring his front legs down, but keep his rear end up. Tell him, "Down dog" and keep repeating it. Give him the treat and praise him when he correctly performs. Do this five to seven times for a few minutes each day. If he tries to lie down on top of your arm, use your arm like a wall: Brace him so he can't lay on it.

4. Once he starts responding, keep your left arm under him and have him follow the treat lure into the Upward Dog position. Move the treat forward a little bit, then slide your left arm forward and under his chest.

5. As you slide your left arm forward, start bringing the treat up and above his head, but not directly above his head. This will force him to stretch his head up and lean forward into the treat, with his chest up and his hindquarters stretched out behind him. Repeat over and over again, "Up dog" throughout and praising him when he performs.

6. Repeat several times a day for five to seven days.

SAY YOUR PRAYERS ★

Ever since I was a little girl this has been my favorite dog trick. My golden retriever Muffin looked so sweet doing this trick. If you are having trouble getting your children to say their prayers at night, watching Rover say his might be the perfect motivation. If you really want to impress your friends add, "Close your eyes" to the end of this trick!

⊕ **HAND SIGNAL**
✎ **VERBAL CUE:** "Say your prayers"
✿ **TOOLS:** Praise and Treats
⊙ **AVG. TIME:** 5-7 Days
✛ **DIFFICULTY:** Intermediate

STEP-BY-STEP

1. Sit in a chair with your dog sitting in front of you, facing you. Pat your knees and tell him to put "Paws up" (sidebar page 19), one on each knee. Praise him.

Sit in a chair, pat your knees and say, "Paws up."

2. Hold a tiny treat in your hand. Tell him, "Say your prayers." As you say the command, take your hand with the treat, lower it to under his chest and from there move it to between your knees. You must include lowering the treat under his chest, as you want your hand low enough that he has to bow his head to get the treat. Tell him, "Head down, say your prayers" (Head Down, page 52). Praise and treat him when he gets it right.

3. Once he has mastered Head Down, slowly inch his legs forward while his head is down, one small increment at a time. Do this very slowly so he gets used to the correct positioning. Praise him when his feet are in the right place.

4. Repeat several times a day for five to seven days.

Slowly stretch his legs forward, one small movement at a time.

 ADVICE FROM THE EXPERT

Use a quiet, calm tone for the commands and the praise. This is a pose where you want your dog to relax, so don't use an excited, happy tone of voice.

PROBLEM SOLVING

Problem: Your dog doesn't keep his head down.

Solution: Brush up on Head Down (page 52) and add Stay (page 11) if necessary in order to achieve the full look of Say Your Prayers.

Here's the position you're aiming for: paws stretched forward and head down.

★ WALK ON HIND LEGS ★ FORWARD AND BACKWARD

○ **HAND SIGNAL**

🖐 **VERBAL CUE:** "Forward, Backward"

⚙ **TOOLS:** Praise and Treats

🕐 **AVG. TIME:** 7-10 Days

✛ **DIFFICULTY:** Intermediate

Who's the next contestant on "Dancing with the Stars"? Why Rover, of course! Just imagine your dog on his hind legs. Watch him cha-cha forward, then back. Advance to Pirouette (page 80) and then the dance moves in Chapter 6 (page 117) and you're sure to garner tens from all the celebrity judges!

Keep this in mind: Any trick that requires standing on the back legs is easier to teach a smaller dog than a large one, as most big dogs are heavier in the chest. This doesn't mean it can't be done, but it may require more patience on your part to ensure Rover builds up the strength and balance to hold the move.

STEP-BY-STEP

1. Hold a treat in your hand. Have Rover come up on his hind legs saying, "Dance" (Walk on Hind Legs, page 20) and steady himself.

2. Once he's steady start moving the treat forward or backward. Watch your dog carefully. His body language will tell you if it's easier for him to walk forward or backward. Most dogs walk forward first. If your dog goes backward first, start with backward (step 4).

Have your dog come up on his hind legs.

> 🏅 **ADVICE FROM THE EXPERT**
> It may seem obvious, but your dog should be able to stand on his hind legs reliably in order to learn this trick or any other dance-related move.

3. As you move very slowly away from him, lure him towards you with the treat. Use the command, "Dance forward." Do it very slowly and let him nibble as he goes. It's important not to push him too hard too soon. If he takes even one or two steps forward stop and give him lots of praise.

4. To teach Backward, move toward him and say, "Dance backward." Again, progress very slowly, praising after even one step.

5. Practice three to five times a day for seven to ten days.

Move the treat forward to encourage him to walk forward.

Eventually Rover will walk forward without the treat as a reward.

🦴 PROBLEM SOLVING

Problem: Your dog is jumping to get the treat rather than balancing correctly.

Solution: Lower your hand to the right level. The treat should be right in front of his face. Experiment as needed with the position of the treat that fits your dog correctly.

★ PIROUETTE ★

HAND SIGNAL
VERBAL CUE: "Spin"
TOOLS: Praise and Treats
AVG. TIME: 5-7 Days
DIFFICULTY: Intermediate

The word "pirouette" is French and means "spinning top." My doggie-style version of this move won't have Rover spinning on one toe like a ballerina, but any twirling canine is sure to elicit claps and whistles. This is also a great trick for transitioning between other moves. As soon as Rover finishes Roll Over (page 58), have him stand up and twirl before moving to Shake Your Body (page 59) or Weave Cones (page 90).

Your dog should be able to stand and walk forward on his hind legs (page 78) in order to learn this trick. You're luring him to move right or left as he walks forward, then speeding up that movement to create a pirouette.

STEP-BY-STEP

1. Hold a treat in your hand. Have Rover come up on his hind legs and steady himself, using the command, "Dance." (Walk on Hind Legs, page 20)

2. Lure him to move to the left or right with the treat. Take care not to move the treat hard right or hard left, but in an arc to his left or right. Move very slowly and keep the treat steady, not too low and not too high.

Once your dog is steady, lure him to the left or right.

Use the command "Spin" as he learns to continue moving his body in a circle.

Lay on the praise as he finishes his pirouette.

3. Each time you practice, move him a little bit more in a circle and say, "Spin!" When he finishes a pirouette, heap on the praise.

4. Practice two to three times a day for five to seven days.

 ADVICE FROM THE EXPERT

Remember that where the head goes, the body will follow. The key in training this trick is to make sure Rover is steady and balanced enough to turn his feet at the same time he turns his head.

PROBLEM SOLVING

Problem: Rover drops out of the standing position once you start luring him to the right or left.

Solution: Chances are you're moving too quickly. Start over with very slow movements. Rover will drop out of the standing position if he's not comfortable, so use a very slow progression into your circular movement.

PUSH A CARRIAGE

HAND SIGNAL

VERBAL CUE: "Push the cart"

TOOLS: Praise and Treats

AVG. TIME: 2-3 Weeks

DIFFICULTY: Advanced

Here's a classic trick pulled right from the big top: Rover pushing a kiddie-sized shopping cart! You can imagine another variation on this: your dog, wearing a dress and pushing his baby doll in the carriage. If you want to get really creative and you've got the right props, dress a smaller dog as the baby and have your pooches perform together!

Before you teach this trick make sure Rover has mastered Paws Up (sidebar page 19) and Walk on Hind Legs Forward (page 78). It's also essential to set up your props correctly. Whatever your dog is pushing has to contain something, such as books or bricks, to balance his weight. Otherwise the carriage will tip backwards towards Rover as soon as he puts his paws up. This is especially true if you're using a lighter-weight, kiddie-style shopping cart or toy baby carriage.

STEP-BY-STEP

1. Begin using a piece of PVC pipe instead of a carriage. Stand facing your dog, holding the pipe. Lower the pipe and tell him, "Paws up." Once he has his paws up on the pipe, give him praise and/or a treat. Stroke his head with one hand while holding the pipe with the other hand and tell him, "Good dog, Push the cart."

Start by having your dog do Paws Up on a piece of plastic pipe.

Have your dog fetch an object.

Tell him, "Drop It" in the carriage.

Give him the cue for "Push the cart."

2. Start walking backwards and tell him, "Push the cart." Walk slowly. You don't want to walk too quickly if he's not steady on his feet.

3. Practice this with a pipe six to eight times for a few days, praising him and giving him a treat when he does it.

4. Once he's mastered pushing the pipe, transition to saying, "Paws up" on the baby carriage or shopping cart. Move slowly. Hold the cart steady (or put a brick in front of it) while he gets used to Paws Up on the cart, and praise him and give him a treat when he performs.

5. Introduce movement very slowly to build up his confidence over time. As soon as he's used to Paws Up on the cart, encourage him to move the cart forward by saying, "Push the cart" and praising when he does. You may want to use your hand to steady the cart the first few times he practices this.

6. Practice three to five times a day for several weeks, until the dog reliably performs.

7. Optional: You can have your dog fetch items and drop them in the cart before he starts pushing. To do this, teach him the object name and have him fetch it (Name That Thingamajig, page 33; Fetch, page 31), then point to the cart and tell him, "Drop it" (page 13). Repeat this sequence a few times a day before you put the entire trick together.

 PROBLEM SOLVING

Problem: Your dog puts his paws up, but then drops down after a few seconds.

Solution: Chances are Rover doesn't have the muscle strength to stay up any longer, or he's losing interest. If it's the first, spend more time with him in Paws Up position to build endurance. If it's the second, you've got to reengage with him and keep his interest. Make sure you're laser-focused on him and he on you. Use a happy voice and make it clear by your tone that you're having fun and you want him to as well!

ADVICE FROM THE EXPERT

This trick is best taught on carpet, not a wood floor (too slick) or lawn (too bumpy). Rover needs the right combination of smooth surface and traction to successfully push the carriage.

★ CLOSE YOUR EYES ★

HAND SIGNAL
VERBAL CUE: "Close your eyes"
TOOLS: Praise
AVG. TIME: 5-7 Days
DIFFICULTY: Beginner

"Close your eyes." Who doesn't love hearing those words just before someone hands them a gift? You can combine this trick with that element of surprise for a fun and entertaining trick, or take it in a different direction and link the Close Your Eyes command to a make-believe hypnosis session. After Rover closes his eyes, continue this scenario by asking funny questions and having him Nod Yes (page 54) or Shake his Head No (page 55).

STEP-BY-STEP

1. Get your dog into a very relaxed state. As he starts to fall asleep next to you, tell him quietly, "Close your eyes."

2. Progress to gently stroking between his eyes in a very light, soothing manner with your index finger. Say, "Close your eyes, close your eyes." Praise him when he does.

3. Alternatively, sit facing your dog and hold his head with one hand under his muzzle, cradling his head. Use the other hand to stroke his head from above. As you stroke his head tell him "Close your eyes, close your eyes." Praise him when he does. Eventually step away from him and start giving the command without touching him. Continue to praise him.

4. Practice three to five times a day for five to seven days.

ADVICE FROM THE EXPERT

This is a trick that's easy to teach by catching your dog as he falls asleep. Don't use the clicker or treats, as that will cause him to open his eyes and pop back up.

PROBLEM SOLVING

Problem: Rover can't settle down enough to close his eyes.

Solution: If you want your dog to be calm you've got to be calm. Use a very soft voice and sit in a quiet environment to teach this trick. Remove any unforeseen distractions, such as a ringing phone or doorbell that will wake up Rover!

★ PLAY OSTRICH ★

Here's an entertaining trick along the lines of Peekaboo (page 122).
Once Rover has mastered peeking out from under a pillow you can
use a blanket, a chair and so on.

⊕ HAND SIGNAL
✍ VERBAL CUE: "Hide your head"
✿ TOOLS: Treats
⊕ AVG. TIME: 5-7 Days
✚ DIFFICULTY: Beginner

STEP-BY-STEP

1. Put a lightweight pillow on a sofa or, for a smaller dog, on the floor. Put a treat under the pillow and tell him, "Find it!" (page 24).

2. Once he sticks his head under the pillow say, "Hide your head, stay" (Stay, page 11). Then release, praise him and give him the treat.

3. Repeat this three to five times the first session. With each session after that make him stay longer under the pillow. Finally, stop using the Stay command and just say, "Hide your head."

4. Practice three to five times a day for five to seven days.

 ADVICE FROM THE EXPERT

Use a pillow that is light enough that your dog can stick his head under it and not feel suffocated, but also big and soft enough that he can't just push it aside to get the treat.

🦴 PROBLEM SOLVING

Problem: Your dog grabs the treat and goes.

Solution: Rover must associate putting his head close to/ under the pillow with the command Hide Your Head, rather than just Find It (page 24). Don't make it too hard for him to get the treat, and experiment with a large, floppy pillow that he can't toss aside. Another idea: Use the clicker to click when he and the pillow are in the exact position you want.

★ ROLL A BARREL ★

HAND SIGNAL
VERBAL CUE: "Roll forward, Roll backward"
TOOLS: Praise and Treats
AVG. TIME: 3-4 Weeks
DIFFICULTY: Advanced

This is definitely a more advanced trick. Imagine those circus dogs rolling their barrels in the center ring! That's not a move they learned overnight—this one may take a couple of a weeks for Rover to master. But with patience and the right barrel most any dog can learn to ride a barrel and propel it forward. This trick will really impress your audience!

Keep these tips in mind: Use a big barrel to start, about the size of a trash can. The barrel should be open on one end. This way you can grab onto it and dictate how fast or slow it rolls. Once Rover is on top of the barrel hold him by the collar until he learns to balance so he can't jump or fall off.

STEP-BY-STEP

1. Tap the barrel and tell your dog, "Paws up" (sidebar page 19). Once he's placed his forelegs up on the barrel give him praise and a treat.

2. Move the barrel back and forth a few inches so he knows it moves.

 ADVICE FROM THE EXPERT
The key here: Make sure your dog is very comfortable on the barrel without any movement before you progress to rolling. This trick takes patience so don't rush the process.

Put a brick in front of the barrel. Lift up Rover's hindquarters and place them on the barrel.

Start rolling it very slowly while you move each of his feet.

When you want him to learn to move the barrel backwards, tap just behind his paws.

🦴 PROBLEM SOLVING

Problem: Rover doesn't seem to grasp the idea of rolling by moving his feet.

Solution: If you move the barrel just a smidgen he will move his feet in order to stay balanced. Use a helper if you need to so you can hold his collar to prevent him from falling off. Use lots of praise and encouragement to solidify what you're looking for.

Problem: Your little dog can't get onto the big barrel.

Solution: You can start his training with a smaller barrel, but keep in mind that the larger the surface area, the easier it will be for any dog to balance. You can also pick up your mini-canine and put him on the barrel to start.

3. Put a brick in front of the barrel so it won't roll forward. Repeat, "Paws up." Lift up his hindquarters and place them on the barrel. Repeat this until he's comfortable having all four feet on the barrel. Eventually you can progress to using the command Hup (page 28) to get him on the barrel.

4. Once he's okay with having four feet on the barrel, you can start rolling it very slowly while you move each of his feet. Hold him by the collar so he doesn't fall off. Tap the front of his paws, which will make him move them backwards, causing the barrel to move forward. Say, "Roll forward."

5. When you want him to learn to move the barrel backwards, tap just behind his paws, which will encourage him to move his feet forward. Say, "Roll backward."

6. Teach him to move forward and backward two or three paces at a time. Repeat each section of this training just a few times and then encourage Rover to get off the barrel.

7. Let him learn on his own that the barrel moves forward and backwards. Once he has gone back and forth a few times you can increase the distance that he rolls the barrel.

8. Practice three to five times a day for several weeks, until your dog reliably performs.

★ ARMY CRAWL ★

- ● **HAND SIGNAL**
- ✋ **VERBAL CUE:** "Crawl"
- ⚙ **TOOLS:** Praise and Treats
- ⏱ **AVG. TIME:** 5-7 Days
- ✚ **DIFFICULTY:** Intermediate

I learned this trick from my father, who served with the infamous 26th Infantry Dog Scout Platoon during the Korean War. This group of highly specialized military dogs was trained to go over, under and through obstacles such as barbed wire, water and footbridges and to ride in vehicles and aircraft. Have some fun with this trick. Use it to create a military-themed skit in combination with moves such as Duck and Cover (page 89) and Fake Limp (page 161).

STEP-BY-STEP

1. Place your dog into a Down position (page 14). Hold a treat on the ground between his forelegs, then slowly slide it away from him.

2. As you slide it away from him back up slowly and quietly say, "Crawl."

3. Give him the opportunity to move forward one pace at a time. The first time out, once he crawls three paces, give him the treat and do it again.

4. Each time have him crawl further and further before you release and praise him. Eventually stop giving him treats and instead use the hand signal while saying, "Crawl."

5. Practice two to three times a day for five to seven days.

Hold a treat on the ground between his legs and slowly slide it away from him. As you slide it away say "Crawl."

🏅 ADVICE FROM THE EXPERT

Retrievers are really good at this trick, but if you're not training a natural-born crawler try bringing your hand very slowly along the ground. Let him nibble at the treat or give him tiny pieces as he moves forward. Don't let him have the full treat unless he's truly crawling.

DUCK AND COVER

This is a great trick to use with a kid as the ringmaster. Once Rover has mastered the verbal command you can have the child wave or pretend to shoot a toy gun to elicit the movement. For a more advanced version of the trick, insert yourself into the mix and go down onto the ground with Rover when you say, "Cover." Tip: Your dog should be well-versed in Down (page 14) to learn this trick.

STEP-BY-STEP

1. As you walk with your dog in the heel position (sidebar, page 12), slide your left hand down the leash towards his collar and push him down to the ground saying, "Down, Cover."

2. Once he gets down, manipulate one paw and front leg to cover his eyes while you say "Cover." Praise him and give him a treat. Once he reliably performs, progress to using the Cover command alone.

3. Repeat this three to five times a day. By the fifth day he should quickly Duck and Cover.

 ADVICE FROM THE EXPERT

To make this trick really effective you'll want to get Rover into the Down position as quickly as possible.

PROBLEM SOLVING

Problem: You want to teach the advanced move, where you also drop to the ground, but your dog is confused by your participation.

Solution: Keep in mind that many of the tricks in this book have you as the commander, not the participant. If he looks at you inquisitively or hesitates give him plenty of praise and lots of loving pats.

★ WEAVE CONES ★

⊙ HAND SIGNAL
ℬ VERBAL CUE: "Weave"
✿ TOOLS: Treats and Praise
⏱ AVG. TIME: 7-10 Days
✛ DIFFICULTY: Advanced

If you've ever thought of training Rover in agility, this is the trick! In a true agility performance the dog moves through a course that includes obstacles such as poles, teeter-totters (page 92) or tunnels. The dog is scored on time and/or accuracy, and the trainer can only use his voice, body language or hand signals to direct the dog. Talk about a true team effort! If Rover quickly catches on to this trick, you can combine any number of moves that involve obstacles (e.g., Jump over Another Dog, page 94) for an exciting and impressive performance.

STEP-BY-STEP

1. Start with five cones. Using a treat, lure your dog to go outside of the first cone.

Use the treat to lure him around the cone.

Repeat the process around the second cone.

2. As he goes around the first cone, lure him towards you with the treat, then reward and praise. Repeat again with the next cone, blocking him from going anywhere but around the cone. Make a big movement indicating he should come towards you and keep up eye contact.

3. Repeat with each cone. Give him lots of praise and repeat.

4. Practice all five cones three to five times a day for seven to ten days.

Keep eye contact as he learns to weave.

 ADVICE FROM THE EXPERT

The key to success when teaching this trick is your body language and alignment. You'll need to use your body language as well as the treat to guide him. Stay alongside him as you teach him how to weave, one cone at a time.

Don't start with the cones 3 feet/0.9 m apart. Begin teaching this trick with the cones positioned about 18 inches/46 cm apart, then progress from there.

PROBLEM SOLVING

Problem: Your dog skips out of the weaving motion.

Solution: Use your left leg and/or your entire body to block him from moving anywhere else but outside of the cone. You can also put him on a leash to keep him close to the cones.

Use your legs to block him if needed.

TEETER-TOTTER ★

● **HAND SIGNAL**
🐾 **VERBAL CUE:** "Teeter"
⚙ **TOOLS:** Praise and Treats
🕐 **AVG. TIME:** 2-3 Weeks
✚ **DIFFICULTY:** Advanced

This trick isn't about fun at the playground, though the prop is the same. This trick will show off Rover's balance and agility skills as he walks up one side of a teeter-totter, balances for a few seconds at the top and walks down the opposite side. As with Weave Cones (page 90), this trick is a classic component of the agility course. If you're looking for an exciting performance for your backyard, this is a great move to string together with other tricks.

You will need a teeter-totter to teach and perform this trick. There's no need to purchase anything special. You can make a low-rise teeter-totter by balancing a 5 or 6 foot/1.5 or 1.8-m two-by-four/four-by-two over a small object such as a piece of firewood. The advanced version of this trick simply involves raising the height of the middle section and lengthening the period of balance at the top.

STEP-BY-STEP

1. Using a treat, lure your dog onto the teeter-totter. The dog should be on the left side heel position.

Lure him onto the teeter-totter.

Hold him steady as he starts to climb.

Spot him as he crosses the middle and his weight shifts.

Praise him as he comes off the teeter-totter

 ADVICE FROM THE EXPERT

Be patient—this trick takes time to train—and make your dog's safety your priority. The middle section, in particular, takes time to teach. Your dog has to learn that it's his weight that shifts the teeter-totter from one side to another, and that he's not going to fall off as the board under his feet moves. Stay by his side as long as needed in order to ensure his safety and build his confidence.

PROBLEM SOLVING

Problem: Rover is too nervous to walk up the angled plank.

Solution: Teach your dog to walk across the plank while it's laying flat on the ground. Once he's mastered that you can create a low teeter-totter, with the lowest height possible at the middle section. Eventually you can raise the height of the teeter-totter.

2. As he starts to approach the middle, hold the teeter-totter steady with one hand and hold him steady with your other hand.

3. Hold the teeter-totter flat as he crosses the middle.

4. Slowly let the teeter-totter go down only as he is crossing the middle and learning to shift his weight. Continue spotting him and holding him steady as the teeter-totter shifts down. Give him lots and lots of praise and treats when he gets to the end.

5. Practice three to five times a day for two to three weeks.

★ JUMP OVER ★ ANOTHER DOG

- ⊕ **HAND SIGNAL**
- ✍ **VERBAL CUE:** "Hup"
- ✿ **TOOLS:** Praise
- ⏱ **AVG. TIME:** 7-10 Days
- ✚ **DIFFICULTY:** Advanced

There's an entire category of fun and exciting tricks that involve Rover working with another dog or even two dogs, as shown here. These tricks have great entertainment value but require a pair of well-trained dogs, so that's your starting point. Once Rover has mastered this trick or others such as Walk Another Dog (page 98), be creative and transform any number of tricks in this book into dual-dog versions. What a hoot! Imagine Duck and Cover (page 89) with two dogs!

You'll need one to two additional dogs for this trick. The dogs in the Down position (page 14) must be used to people walking, running and jumping over them. And your dog should be able to Hup (page 28) over a broad object.

STEP-BY-STEP

1. Put the additional dogs in Down-Stay (page 14). Show your dog the obstacle you want him to jump.

Show your dog the obstacle he's going to jump.

Run towards the jump alongside your dog.

Encourage him and say, "Hup" as he leaps.

Just jumping over one dog is impressive too!

 ADVICE FROM THE EXPERT

Not only do you need a pair of well-trained dogs for training this trick, but also your canine companions should know and enjoy each other. They might not associate outside the office, so to speak, but you're asking them to work together, so familiarity is key.

PROBLEM SOLVING

Problem: You can imagine the most common problem with this trick: One of the dogs moves and/or disrupts the trick.

Solution: One dog needs to love jumping, and not just jumping but transporting himself over high and broad objects. The additional dogs need a rock-solid Down-Stay (page 14). You can practice this with them individually by having people and kids walk, run and hop over them and rewarding their statue-like stillness.

2. Run the jumping dog at a swift pace towards the additional dogs. As he jumps, use the command Hup (page 28). Once he's over the down dogs, give him lots of praise.

3. Repeat this ten to twelve times the first time, then three to five times a day for seven to ten days.

★ CRAWL UNDER ANOTHER DOG ★

⊕ **HAND SIGNAL**
🗩 **VERBAL CUE:** "Crawl"
⚙ **TOOLS:** Praise and Treats
🕐 **AVG. TIME:** 5-7 Days
➕ **DIFFICULTY:** Advanced

Need another multiple-dog trick for your performance? Here's your next entertaining move: one dog standing perfectly still while another crawls under him. I love the effect this creates. The teamwork alone is impressive, let alone the individual tricks the dogs need to master to make this work! As mentioned in other dual-dog tricks, you can build a wonderful performance by combining this trick with tandem tricks. Imagine your dogs simultaneously performing tricks like synchronized swimmers. Or be creative and insert yourself as the ringmaster. Have one dog perform a single trick, have the second dog perform a single trick, then insert yourself and have both dogs perform the same trick with you, such as Jump over Me (page 102) or Jump into My Arms (Hup, step 9, page 29).

STEP-BY-STEP

1. Set up the standing dog in a Stand-Stay position (Stay, step 9, page 11).

2. Position the crawling dog perpendicular to the standing dog. Point to the space under the standing dog and say, "Crawl."

Point to where you want the crawling dog to go.

Lure the crawling dog along with a treat.

Getting your dog under the other dog is a big step, even if he's not crawling.

Praise both dogs when the trick is done!

 ADVICE FROM THE EXPERT

You'll need two dogs for training this trick: One pooch that is tall and long enough for the second dog to crawl under him. The standing dog must be very good at Stand-Stay (Stay, step 9, page 11) and the second dog must know how to crawl (Army Crawl, page 88) consistently and without hesitation.

PROBLEM SOLVING

Problem: Both dogs know their individual roles, but they hesitate or balk when you try to combine their moves.

Solution: Step back and make sure you've set up the dogs to work as a team. Do the dogs know each other? Are they friendly to each other? You can easily build on this bond by introducing regular play sessions with just your pair of entertainers. Are you the ringmaster for each? Make solid eye contact with both dogs individually, and be sure to serve up the praise or reward them with treats equally. Eventually they'll come to understand that pleasing you together is key to the reward.

3. Hold a treat on the other side to lure him through. Make sure your standing dog is not highly motivated by food or he might break the Stand-Stay to grab the treat.

4. Once the crawling dog gets through, give both dogs a treat and praise.

5. Practice this one to three times the first time. Repeat three to five times for five to seven days.

★ WALK ANOTHER DOG ★

⊕ HAND SIGNAL
🐾 VERBAL CUE: "Walk the dog"
✿ TOOLS: Praise
⊙ AVG. TIME: 2-3 Weeks
✚ DIFFICULTY: Advanced

Any move that uses two dogs is sure to bring out some smiles. Add in the fact that you're asking Rover to perform a human action and the irony of one dog walking another and you've nailed the entertainment factor.

That said, this is not a trick for beginners. Before you can teach this trick both dogs need a solid Heel in place (sidebar, page 12). If they don't know how to heel then put this training on hold and start there. Once they've nailed Heel, you will kick off the training for this trick by teaching them how to walk in a brace.

"Brace" is a category of competition where a single handler shows two dogs at the same time. The two dogs typically enter the ring side by side and are judged on their ability to act as a pair.

STEP-BY-STEP

1. Put both leashed dogs in the Heel position (sidebar, page 12), side by side, on your left side.

2. Put the inside dog's leash in your right hand. Put the outside dog's leash in your left hand. Tell both dogs, "Let's walk."

3. If the dogs want to switch sides, they will quickly switch on their own. If they do, allow it. You want to let them choose the side where they will be content walking next to one another.

4. Practice this several times a day for a few days before advancing.

 ADVICE FROM THE EXPERT

There are two key steps to success with this trick: Both dogs have to know how to heel very well. Second, both dogs have to master the concept of "brace." Once you've got those building blocks in place it's all fun and games!

If they're both good at holding objects, try the more advanced version of this trick: Give them both leashes and let them walk each other!

Put the leash on the first dog, then tell the second dog to take it.

Once the second dog has picked up the leash, tell him, "Walk."

Walk ahead and say, "Come."

Eventually you can have the dogs try it on their own.

5. When you're ready to teach them "Walk the dog," position the dogs side by side with one attached to a leash. Tell one dog, "Take it" (sidebar, page 45) and place the leash in his mouth. Tell him, "Walk the dog." It doesn't matter which dog holds the leash in this trick, the dog on the outside or the dog on the inside. Select the dog that's more comfortable holding the leash.

6. Walk ahead of the dogs and say, "Come." This is one of those tricks where the reward is in the work. Go for several paces and then give them lots of praise.

7. Repeat, each time increasing the distance that both dogs walk. Eventually you can advance to the dogs walking alone.

🦴 PROBLEM SOLVING

Problem: Rover seems overwhelmed by holding the leash and walking and working next to a second dog.

Solution: Break this trick down into several parts and take your time mastering each section before you string them all together. For example, let him get used to holding the leash in his mouth before you have him move alongside his canine companion.

★ SHELL GAME ★

- **HAND SIGNAL**
- **VERBAL CUE:** "Find the treat"
- **TOOLS:** Praise and Treats
- **AVG. TIME:** 5-7 Days
- **DIFFICULTY:** Intermediate

If you ever played magician as a child you'll remember this trick: Place an object under one of three shells, move the shells around to mix things up, then impress your audience by lifting up the correct shell to reveal the object! This canine version is equally entertaining. Just have Rover pick the correct shell!

You'll need three small plastic flowerpots or cups, a smooth surface and strong-smelling treats for training this trick.

STEP-BY-STEP

1. Set the three flowerpots or cups upside down on a smooth surface. Put your dog in a Sit-Stay (page 11).

2. Show him the treat, then place it under one of the flowerpots.

Put a treat under one of the pots.

3. Shuffle the pots around and stop. Tell your dog, "Find the treat" and show your dog the pots. He may knock the correct flowerpot over with his nose or even his paw.

4. Once he finds the right pot, let him eat the treat and give him lots of praise.

5. Practice three to five times a day for five to seven days.

Show your dogs the pots and tell him, "Find the treat."

 ADVICE FROM THE EXPERT

What constitutes a strong-smelling treat? A slice of hot dog, that's what!

PROBLEM SOLVING

Problem: Your dog can identify the right flowerpot, but everything's getting knocked over!

Solution: Refining the presentation requires refining your dog's behavior. If he's pawing at all of the pots or is not accustomed to using his nose, go back to Find It (page 24) and review the nose work. Layer in the commands for Touch It (page 22) or Bump (page 27) if needed.

Praise him when he gets it right!

JUMP OVER ME

HAND SIGNAL
VERBAL CUE: "Hup"
TOOLS: Praise
AVG. TIME: 5-7 Days
DIFFICULTY: Intermediate

If your dog loves to jump, let him: Lay on your stomach or your back to make yourself an easy obstacle! Once Rover has mastered this trick you can make it a dual-dog version with both dogs jumping at the same time, or one following the other. What a hoot!

STEP-BY-STEP

1. Lie face down on the floor. Have a helper show the dog that you want him to jump over you.

2. Have the helper run the jumping dog at a swift pace towards you. Once he's over you, give him lots of praise. Use the command Hup (page 28) as he jumps.

3. Repeat this ten to twelve times the first time.

4. To advance, try having him jump over you while you're face up, or add another person.

ADVICE FROM THE EXPERT

Your helper needs to be someone your dog knows and obeys, particularly because they're in the command position for this trick.

PROBLEM SOLVING

Problem: Your dog seems distracted by you being a part of the trick.

Solution: Be sure your helper is someone your dog is familiar with. Keep Rover laser-focused on the task at hand by using a leash and/or treat if needed.

★ CHAPTER FIVE ★

HELP ME OUT

Your dog's a member of your family, right? Everyone in my family shares the workload. We take turns doing the dishes, we empty the trash and we fold the laundry for each other. This chapter will give you a fun and varied list of helper tasks for Rover, from Sort the Laundry (page 106) to Pick up Your Toys (page 112) and even Hold the Dustpan (page 114).

And all helpers deserve a reward, right? Once your dog is consistently doing his share around the house and/or yard, be sure to give him the doggie-style equivalent of a weekly allowance. A new toy? An extra-long walk in the woods? Or maybe just the opportunity to snuggle up close for extra loving. Whatever the reward, make it count.

And don't forget: Too much work and no play makes Jack a dull boy. Remember to have fun as you and Rover do your chores. Even whistle while you work!

★ RING THE DOORBELL ★

- **HAND SIGNAL**
- **VERBAL CUE:** "Ring the bell"
- **TOOLS:** Treats
- **AVG. TIME:** 5-7 Days
- **DIFFICULTY:** Advanced

Many dogs bark when the doorbell rings, and some will even bark if they hear a doorbell on the television! But that's no reason not to teach your dog how to Ring the Doorbell, a handy move that's both useful and entertaining.

This isn't a trick for beginners, and it may be more challenging to teach small dogs than larger breeds. For shorter dogs, I recommend hanging bells on the doorknob to teach this trick. Even if you're training a big dog, keep in mind that pressing a doorbell may be difficult. The pads on their feet may not be the right size or the button on the bell may not easily press. If this is the case, either hang bells on the doorknob or get creative: Purchase a freestanding button (office supplies stores sometimes sell them saying "easy" or "no") and affix it to a surface Rover can reach.

STEP-BY-STEP

1. Hold the treat to lure your dog to the bell, and show him the bell. Tell him, "Paws up, touch it, ring the bell" (Paws Up, sidebar page 19; Touch It, page 22). Once he does, give him the treat.

2. Repeat three to five times the first session.

3. Practice three to five times for five to seven days. As you progress drop one of the verbal cues, then another, so he will complete the trick on his own with only the Ring the Bell command.

🎖 ADVICE FROM THE EXPERT

Your dog will need to know Paws Up (sidebar, page 19) and Touch It (page 22) before you teach this trick. The key is to start with a cue that your dog already knows, then add the new verbal command to bridge and rename the action.

🦴 PROBLEM SOLVING

Problem: Your dog can ring the doorbell but barks when he hears it.

Solution: Review the directions for Stop Barking (Speak: Advice from the Expert, page 60).

BRING ME FLOWERS

Who doesn't love getting flowers? Now Rover can play a part in delivering a special gift! Once he's mastered this trick he can deliver any number of items, from your husband's slippers and newspaper to a magazine, blanket or pillow!

⊙ HAND SIGNAL
✋ VERBAL CUE: "Carry flowers"
✿ TOOLS: Praise
⊙ AVG. TIME: 5-7 Days
✚ DIFFICULTY: Intermediate

STEP-BY-STEP

1. Give the flowers to your dog and say, "Take it" (sidebar, page 45). Then tell him "Go to Auntie".

2. Have Auntie call your dog, "Come" (page 12). As soon as your dog gets to Auntie have her give him lots of praise.

3. Repeat this several times, then say, "Go to Auntie, carry flowers." Over time transition to the Carry Flowers command alone.

4. Practice several times a day for five to seven days.

🏅 ADVICE FROM THE EXPERT

If your dog is going to carry an actual bouquet something needs to hold the flowers together (e.g., rubber band, paper or plastic sleeve). Familiarize your dog with the packaging—think what the plastic smells like, what it will sound like when he grabs hold and so on—before you ask him to carry the flowers.

🦴 PROBLEM SOLVING

Problem: Your dog doesn't get the concept of grasping the flowers with his mouth.

Solution: This trick takes time and patience. You can put the flowers in a gift bag, but remember you have to familiarize Rover with the bag, the handles and how to carry it. Better to start with the flowers and build from there.

★ SORT THE LAUNDRY ★

HAND SIGNAL
VERBAL CUE: "Fetch the darks" and "Fetch the lights"
TOOLS: Praise
AVG. TIME: 7-10 Days
DIFFICULTY: Advanced

We know Rover can't put the soap in the washing machine and start the cycle, but there's no reason why he can't still help with the laundry! Here's an easy-to-teach task that's sure to impress your houseguests. It's a variation of Fetch (page 31) and Drop It (page 13), but using your clean socks or t-shirts instead of a stick or a ball.

Once he's mastered this trick, you can cook up other variations on Fetch and Drop It, such as Pick up Your Toys (page 112) or pick up the pillows. You can even use Rover's newfound skill in the yard. Have him pick up all the sticks and drop them in a pile, then give him one to chew on as a reward!

STEP-BY-STEP

1. Pile the clothes on the floor. Point to the pile of laundry. Pick up something dark and tell him, "Take it, dark, fetch, drop it."

2. While he is getting the dark article of clothing, point to where you want him to bring it, then tell him, "Drop it." Once he does, give him lots of love and praise.

Point to the pile of laundry. Tell your dog to take a dark piece of clothing.

Once he comes to where you want him to bring it, tell him, "Drop it."

3. Repeat five times with something dark.

4. Repeat the process with something light and tell him, "Take it, light, fetch, drop it."

5. Once he starts doing lights and darks with reliability you can shorten the command to "Fetch the darks" or "Fetch the lights."

6. Practice three to five times a day for seven to ten days.

 ADVICE FROM THE EXPERT

Make sure your dog is really good at fetching things and dropping them where you want them before you train this trick. As with any move that combines other moves, the foundational steps are critical for success.

PROBLEM SOLVING

Problem: Your dog picks up a pair of pants and drags them. As he's dragging the pants he steps on them, then gets frustrated and/or distracted.

Solution: Start the training with something very small, like a sock, then build up to a pair of boxer shorts or T-shirt.

Repeat with a light-colored article of clothing.

★ TUCK ANOTHER ★ DOG IN

● **HAND SIGNAL**
🖐 **VERBAL CUE:** "Tuck another dog in"
⚙ **TOOLS:** Praise
🕐 **AVG. TIME:** 5-7 Days
✛ **DIFFICULTY:** Intermediate

It's a familiar nighttime ritual if you've got kids: Tuck them in and kiss them goodnight. You can create the same routine with Rover, but teach him to tuck another dog in before you kiss both of them goodnight! This is a great ending trick for a skit with a domestic theme, or even as the closing move for a sports- or dance-related set of tricks. Just be sure to tell your dog to close his eyes once he's tucked in!

STEP-BY-STEP

1. Put the first dog in a Down-Stay (page 14) and lay a light-weight baby blanket slightly over him.

Position the dogs with the blanket on one side.

Point to the blanket and tell the second dog "take it."

Once he takes it, tell him, "Tug it."

Repeat the Tug It command until the blanket is all the way over.

ADVICE FROM THE EXPERT

Although this isn't a difficult trick to teach, grasping the concept of pulling a blanket over another dog doesn't come naturally to Rover. Be patient and be creative with the type and/or size of blanket you use.

PROBLEM SOLVING

Problem: Your dog is having trouble pulling the blanket all the way over.

Solution: Make sure Rover is grabbing the middle section of the blanket edge, not the corner.

2. Point to the middle edge of the blanket and tell the second dog, "Take it" (sidebar, page 45). Then tell him, "Tug it" (page 23), repeating the command until the blanket is over the first dog. Then tell him, "Drop it" (page 13) until he lets go.

3. Practice two to three times a day for five to seven days.

★ GO WAKE UP ★
YOUR FRIEND

Once your dog knows everyone's name you can put him to work!
What a great way to wake up: having your dog give you kisses. Plus your
kids will love participating in the training.

⊕ HAND SIGNAL
✍ VERBAL CUE: "Go wake up ____"
✿ TOOLS: Praise and Treats
⊘ AVG. TIME: 5-7 Days
✚ DIFFICULTY: Intermediate

STEP-BY-STEP

1. Have Stephanie get in bed and put a small smear of butter on her cheek.

2. Bring your dog just outside the bedroom and tell her, "Go to Stephanie, go wake up Stephanie!" (Go To, see sidebar)

3. Herd him towards the bedroom, repeating, "Go to Stephanie, go wake up Stephanie."

4. Once he's in the bedroom say, "Find Stephanie" (page 24). Chances are he'll go to your child's face and find the butter to lick off, but if not say, "Kiss Stephanie" (page 64). Have Stephanie give your dog lots of love and praise.

5. Repeat the process, but each time move farther away from the bedroom. After the third day the pattern will be set. Drop, "Go to Stephanie," and simply use "Go wake up Stephanie." After practicing one to two times a day for a week you'll have a new trick.

WHAT'S THE OPPOSITE OF COME? GO TO!

Several tricks in this book require Rover knowing how to "go to" a person he knows by name. This is fun to teach with at least three people.

Start by having everyone gather in a circle and take turns loving your dog. Rub him down, massage him, pet him. Have one person (e.g., Jack) call him. As he calls, give your dog a gentle push towards Jack and say, "Go to Jack." If needed, have Jack say, "Come" (page 12). Once he goes to Jack, make sure Jack gives him lots of praise. Repeat the process with the next person in the circle (e.g., Steven). Tell your dog, "Go to Steven." As your dog figures it out, eliminate the Come command. Practice three to five times a day for five to seven days.

★ TURN THE LIGHTS ★ ON AND OFF

○ **HAND SIGNAL**

🗩 **VERBAL CUE:** "Lights off" and "Lights on"

⚙ **TOOLS:** Praise and Treats

⏱ **AVG. TIME:** 3-4 Weeks

✚ **DIFFICULTY:** Advanced

This trick has a great entertainment factor, but your success is dependent on several important variables, including having the right type of light switch at the right height in the right location. A light switch that's too close to a doorway, for example, will be difficult to use. One that's out of Rover's reach won't work, either. If he can reach the switch with his nose, however, you can substitute Bump (page 27) for Touch it (page 22).

Be patient and have fun, and if you don't have the right setup to train this trick, move to something you know your dog can succeed at.

STEP-BY-STEP

1. Teach Rover Paws Up (sidebar page 19) next to the light switch. Hold a treat just above the height needed to reach the light switch then reward him when he reaches the right height.

2. Next, teach your dog to Bump (page 27) the light switch. Tap the switch and say, "Bump." Practice a few times using "bump" and "lights off," then transition to "lights off" alone. Teaching him the nuanced action of bumping the switch to move it to "off" will take practice and patience.

3. Alternatively, you can can use, "Touch it" (page 22) so he turns the light switch on and off using his paw. For some dogs this will be easier than Bump.

4. Once he masters "lights off" you can move to "lights on." Repeat the process, but show him how to bump the light switch so it moves upwards and use the command "lights on." Again, this will take time and patience.

5. Practice three to five times a day for three to four weeks.

🎖 **ADVICE FROM THE EXPERT**

This trick takes patience and practice. Be flexible and creative. Use your imagination and other commands in this book to help Rover succeed.

★ PICK UP YOUR TOYS ★

HAND SIGNAL
VERBAL CUE: "Pick up your toys"
TOOLS: Praise
AVG. TIME: 5-7 Days
DIFFICULTY: Advanced

Imagine a rainy day: The kids have been playing all day, first with one set of toys and then with another. You hit the point where it's time to clean up. As most parents know, you're more likely to have success with cleanup if you present the chore as a game. The same principle applies with your dog! This canine version of cleanup lets Rover do the work while you supervise ... all in good fun.

In some ways this trick is taught in the same way as Sort the Laundry (page 106), but you'll start by teaching your dog the names of his toys (e.g., bunny, ball) as well as where to drop each thing, such as into a toy box or plastic bin.

STEP-BY-STEP

1. First get your dog interested in a toy by waving it around. Put the toy down and point to it. Teach your dog the name of the toy using Name That Thingamajig (page 33). This step alone may take three to five days. Practice a few times with a small number of items before you add other objects.

Get the dog interested in the toy by waving it around.

Put the toy down and point to it.

Point to the bin and say "Drop it."

Repeat the process with each of Rover's toys.

ADVICE FROM THE EXPERT

Many of the advanced tricks in this book aren't really advanced moves on their own; they're a series of singular tricks put together to create a sequence. This series of tricks requires a good solid Fetch (page 31), Take It (page 45) and Drop It (page 13) for success.

PROBLEM SOLVING

Problem: Your dog picks up a few toys, but then seems overwhelmed and doesn't finish the task.

Solution: Overwhelmed is the operative word here. Chances are he's trying to process too much information at once. Back up and start over with just two or three toys. Be patient and eventually Rover will nail this smaller version of the trick. Once he's comfortable you can increase the number of items you want him to clean up.

2. Stand by the toy box. Have him retrieve each toy (Fetch, page 31) in succession (e.g., "fetch the ball" then "fetch the bunny" then "fetch the bone").

3. Point to the toy box and tell him, "Drop it" (page 13). Each time he picks something up and drops it in the right place, give him praise.

4. Insert the command "Pick up your toys" in the sequence: "Fetch it, drop it, pick up your toys." After he reliably performs, drop Fetch and Drop It.

5. Practice three to five times a day for five to seven days.

★ HOLD THE DUSTPAN ★

Here's another variation on Fetch (page 31) that has entertainment and practical use!

● **HAND SIGNAL**
ॐ **VERBAL CUE:** "Hold the dustpan"
✿ **TOOLS:** Praise
🕐 **AVG. TIME:** 5-7 Days
✚ **DIFFICULTY:** Intermediate

STEP-BY-STEP

1. Teach Rover what the dustpan is using Name That Thingamajig (page 33). Start by giving it to him and letting him hold it in his mouth.

Offer the dustpan to Rover.

2. Transition to putting the dustpan somewhere he can easily find it and say, "Fetch dustpan" (Fetch, page 31). Give him lost of praise when he brings it to you.

3. Use the Drop It command (page 13) to have him drop the dustpan.

4. Practice three to five times a day for five to seven days.

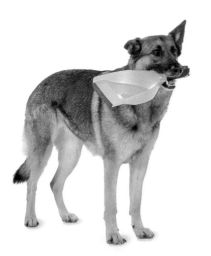

Have him hold it in his mouth.

 ADVICE FROM THE EXPERT

Be sure to use a plastic dustpan, not metal. If you're training a miniature dog, use a dustpan with a hole at the top for hanging. Thread a soft rope or rag through the hole and let your dog drag the dustpan instead of carrying.

PROBLEM SOLVING

Problem: Your dog will fetch the dustpan but drops it immediately.

Solution: The dustpan handle's grooves, which are designed to fit around a broom handle, may feel odd in his mouth. If he drops it immediately, work on getting him used to holding it for short periods. Start at ten seconds, move up to twenty, then forty-five and so on.

Tell your dog "Drop it."

★ GO OUT OF THE ROOM ★

This trick is both entertaining and very practical. You can have some fun while entertaining your guests by sending Rover out of the room. Once he's mastered the trick, change up the command to something like "Dogs are better not seen or heard!" On a practical note, this trick is useful if you break a glass, have just mopped your kitchen floor or spill food, especially any food that's dangerous for dogs, such as chocolate or grapes.

STEP-BY-STEP

1. Start in the middle of the room. Stand behind your dog, keeping him between you and the exit.

2. Tell him, "Go out."

3. Start herding him out of the room. Keep pointing towards the exit and keep moving him towards the exit saying, "Go out, go out, go out."

4. Once he gets to the other side of the exit, give him lots of praise.

5. Repeat this three to five times a day for three days. He may be confused at first but after three days he will understand.

 ADVICE FROM THE EXPERT

Be consistent and patient when teaching this trick and reward him generously once he grasps the concept.

🦴 **PROBLEM SOLVING**

Problem: Your dog doesn't move when you say, "Go out."

Solution: Keep herding him out of the room. If he turns around and follows you back into the room repeat the herding.

★ CHAPTER SIX ★

SING, DANCE AND PLAY GAMES

Sing, dance and play games: If any of those sound like fun, then this is the chapter for you and your dog! You may be wondering, "How in the world am I going to teach my dog to sing?" Have no worries; every dog makes his own variation of crooning sounds, though you may not have noticed or thought about developing your dog's vocal chords. Singing is easy to master, and your dog's performance is sure to earn him oohs, aahs and calls of "Bravo!"

What if your talented canine crooner also wants to dance? All the more fun! Let's teach him a few hops, jumps and hip-swinging moves to fill up his dance card and mix up the talent show. Better yet, have one dog sing while another dances—the possibilities for fun and laughter are endless!

If your dog prefers sports and games to theater arts there are tricks that teach Rover how to play basketball or soccer, go bowling and even swing a baseball bat! Whether we're working with the next Broadway star or a potential Olympic athlete, let's get started training!

★ SING ★

- ⊙ **HAND SIGNAL**
- ℬ **VERBAL CUE:** "Sing"
- ✿ **TOOLS:** Praise
- ⏱ **AVG. TIME:** 7-10 Days
- ✚ **DIFFICULTY:** Advanced

I know, it sounds ridiculous. A singing dog? Although it sounds implausible, it's not, and it's a fabulous trick for eliciting laughs and claps. This was one of my father Captain Haggerty's standbys during his performances on David Letterman's show.

Singing is not that hard to teach, assuming your dog either naturally responds to a trigger with any noise other than barking, or can learn to. As you move through the steps, you'll see I use the word "howl." This means nose to the sky, just like a coyote when he croons. Some Rovers croon in other positions. I've watched Heidi, a sweet and gentle bullmastiff, sing into her owner's ear.

This is a great trick for sled dogs. They are absolute naturals at crooning out a tune. Like many tricks in this book, this is one you have to capture. And you can't use a treat here—he can't sing with his mouth full!

STEP-BY-STEP

1. Identify a trigger for any song-like sound from your dog, for example a fire engine or a high-pitched sound you play for him.

2. Once he starts howling, tell him, "Sing Elvis, Sing." Praise him lavishly.

3. Repeat this whenever you catch him howling. Over time you can play around to help him develop different pitches, and play with your own voice so he'll sing back to you.

4. Practice three to five times a day for seven to ten days.

 ADVICE FROM THE EXPERT

If your dog already howls at a noise such as the fire engine or a particular song, that's great. You just have to capture the trigger, associate it with your verbal cue (sing!) and lay on the praise. Simple as one-two-three!

There are some sounds that elicit howling more than others, though every dog is different. If you want to test a variety of sounds, start with a noise he doesn't hear all the time, such as a whistling siren or a howling coyote.

★ DO YOUR ★ ARITHMETIC

- ⊕ **HAND SIGNAL**
- ✌ **VERBAL CUE:** "Speak"
- ⚙ **TOOLS:** Clicker, Treat and Praise
- ⏱ **AVG. TIME:** 3-4 Weeks
- ✚ **DIFFICULTY:** Advanced

I love this trick, as there so many creative variations. Years ago I taught a dog named Cali to bark out how many times her master, the famous golfer Jack Nicklaus, had won the Masters, the British Open and so on. It was great entertainment!

This trick starts with a fundamental move, Speak (page 16), that can be used for a wide variety of tricks. In this variation you'll teach your dog Do Your Arithmetic, which is as simple as asking "what is two plus two?" and using the hand signal to cue him to bark four times! Once you've mastered the concept together, have Rover bark on cue as you ask him various questions, such as "How many treats did you have?" or "What's our phone number?" (Clearly that second one is for the advanced dog.)

STEP-BY-STEP

1. Once he's mastered Speak (page 16), your dog can bark on cue. Now teach him to bark on cue when you ask different questions. Start with a math problem.

2. Hold a treat up by your face. Say, "What is two plus two?" Use the hand signal for Speak. After he barks four times, click, smile, give him the treat and praise him. The number of barks should depend on how long you hold up the signal.

3. After three to five times he will watch your expression and start to put two and two together (pun intended). Pair your click with your smile and praise.

4. Eventually you'll wean off the click and treat and just use your smile and praise as the reward.

5. You'll also need a signal for when to stop barking. You can teach this using the same technique outlined above.

6. Practice three to five times a day for three to four weeks.

✿ ADVICE FROM THE EXPERT

Start out simple when teaching your dog how to do his arithmetic, such as one plus one equals two, so you can nail the trick before you move on. Introducing your dog to too many concepts at once is only going to confuse him and probably lead to frustration on his part and yours.

★ ELECTRIC SLIDE ★

Here's a group dance that's sure to elicit claps and calls and may even pull your guests out of their seats to join in! This well-known line dance, which originated in the '70s, is typically set to "Electric Boogie" by female reggae singer Marcia Griffiths. Perform this trick on your own, with a group or even as part of a Doggie Dance Moves skit!

◉ **HAND SIGNAL**
ઈ **VERBAL CUE:** "To the right, To the left, forward, backward, Electic Slide"
✿ **TOOLS:** Treats and Clicker
◷ **AVG. TIME:** 3-4 Weeks
✚ **DIFFICULTY:** Advanced

STEP-BY-STEP

1. Use a treat to lure your dog to your left (his right). Say, "To the right," then click and treat. Repeat five to eight times.

2. Once he understands what you want, repeat the process to teach him, "To the left." Practice three to five times a day for four to five days before you put the dance moves together.

3. To do the Electric Slide, start with your dog in a standing position. Tell Rover, "Electric Slide, go to your right" twice. Click and clap your hands.

4. Then say, "Electric Slide, go to your left" twice. Click and clap.

Tell Rover, "Electric Slide, go to your right."

Next, tell him, "Electric Slide, go to your left."

Then tell him, "Electric Slide, forward!"

5. If you have taught your dog Walk on Hind Legs Forward and Back (page 78), use those cues (Dance forward, Dance backward) to teach the next steps.

6. If not, teach Forward and Backward using steps one through four. Replace "to the left" and "to the right" with "to the front" and "to the back," and eventually ending with "Electric Slide, to the front" and "Electric slide, to the back."

7. Practice a few times a day for three to four weeks. Be very patient.

 ADVICE FROM THE EXPERT

The key here is teaching your dog how to go to the right and then go to the left. Remember that when you're facing your dog the direction is the opposite, so when you say right they're going to your left, and so on.

PROBLEM SOLVING

Problem: Rover doesn't get it.

Solution: Like some of the other advanced tricks in this book, Electric Slide requires stringing together several individual moves. If your dog has a problem combining any of the steps, break the dance into smaller combination moves and practice those. Try working on "Electric Slide, go to your left" and "Electric Slide, go to your right" together for one to two weeks. Then work on "Electric Slide, to the front" and "Electric Slide, to the back" for one to two weeks. Last but not least put the four moves together.

Last but not least, "Electric Slide, back up!"

★ HOKEY POKEY ★

HAND SIGNAL
VERBAL CUE: "Hokey pokey"
TOOLS: Clicker, Treats and Praise
AVG. TIME: 2-3 Weeks
DIFFICULTY: Advanced

If you've never done the hokey pokey, you'll need to imagine the moves that accompany these instructions to participants:

You put your right foot in.
You put your right foot out.
You put your right foot in and you shake it all about.
You do the hokey pokey and you turn yourself around.
That's what it's all about!
You put your left foot in.
You put your left foot out.
You put your left foot in and you shake it all about.
You do the hokey pokey and you turn yourself around.
That's what it's all about!

STEP-BY-STEP

1. Put your dog in a Stand-Stay (step 9, page 11) and position a small cone in front of him.

2. Start by teaching him to put his paw in. Point to the cone and tell him, "Hokey pokey, touch it, right" then click and treat. The goal is to get him to Touch It (page 22) (the cone will eventually be removed) with his paw. As you work through this you'll eventually drop the command "touch."

You know the dance moves: "hokey pokey right paw . . ."

Now start with the left paw!

And here's the hokey pokey spin!

ADVICE FROM THE EXPERT

The key to success in training this trick is to break the dance apart into three parts and then chain the three pieces back together once Rover has separately mastered them. In this case, part A comprises steps two and three: hokey pokey right paw and hokey pokey shake. Part B includes steps four and five: hokey pokey left paw and hokey pokey shake. Part C is step nine, hokey pokey spin.

PROBLEM SOLVING

Problem: Your dog doesn't seem to get it.

Solution: Be very patient and give your dog plenty of time for connecting the dots. Make it fun. Use your happy voice and reward every success, no matter how small. If he's still not catching on break it down into tiny pieces and master those before moving on. Keep in mind this is a very advanced trick that may require several weeks to learn.

3. Next tell him "Shake your paw" (page 62) and "Hokey pokey, shake." When he does this, click and treat. The goal here is to have your dog to shake his paw. It doesn't matter if he pulls his foot back after touching the cone and then shakes, or if he moves directly from extending his paw to touch the cone and then shaking. Put the two steps together and practice at least five times each day over four to five days.

4. For the spin part of the dance tell him to Pirouette (page 80) and "Hokey pokey, spin." Click and treat. As before, practice this several times, then eventually drop the Pirouette command and use "Hokey pokey, spin" alone.

5. Combine the three moves, remembering to have your dog do the paw move twice before he spins. Click and treat. After five to ten successions, stop treating each time, but just give a click. Eventually you can remove the click all together and just use the commands.

6. Practice several times a day for two to three weeks. Last but not least, add your other participants (human or canine!) into the dance!

★ PLAY THE PIANO ★

● **HAND SIGNAL**
🐾 **VERBAL CUE:** "Play"
⚙ **TOOLS:** Clicker, Treats and Praise
🕐 **AVG. TIME:** 5-7 Days
✚ **DIFFICULTY:** Intermediate

Who doesn't love the picture of Rover sitting at a miniature piano, tapping away at the keys while crooning along in time? It's a great visual, and you can bring this scene to life using a toy keyboard placed on the floor. Not quite as dramatic as the picture, perhaps, but potentially just as entertaining and certainly easier for your dog to master!

For an advanced version, put two dogs together, one on the keyboards and one singing. You can do this by associating the sound of the key your piano-playing dog plays with the Sing (page 118) or even the Speak (page 16) command. Build up this association to include several keys and soon enough you'll have a full-blown duet!

STEP-BY-STEP

1. Tell your dog, "Paws up" (sidebar page 19) on the keyboard.

2. Tell him, "Touch it, play" (Touch It, page 22) as you take his paw and have it hit a key. Click and treat and praise.

Tell your dog, "Paws up" (sidebar page 19) on the keyboard.

3. Repeat five times the first time. Each time he hits a key, give him a treat. Eventually progress to just clicking and giving praise when he responds to the verbal cue.

4. You will be amazed where this goes. You may start getting sounds, howls and a variety of barks out of your dog!

5. Practice three to five times a day for five to seven days.

Tell him, "Touch it, play" (Touch It, page 22) as you take his paw and have it hit a key. Click and treat and praise.

 ADVICE FROM THE EXPERT

I don't recommend staying on the "treat" portion of this trick too long. If you're familiar with the concept of Pavlov's dog then you know a dog can quickly figure out how to do something (e.g., touch a keyboard) that's rewarded with a treat. Unless you want piano banging all day long, try to move quickly to the clicking phase.

PROBLEM SOLVING

Problem: Rover puts his paw on the keyboard but won't repeat the action.

Solution: Point to another key and say, "Touch it" (page 22). Eventually he'll catch on to the idea of "playing" the keyboard by moving his paws around in return for a treat and, eventually, your praise.

★ CARRY AN EGG ★

This is a great trick that will really impress your friends, especially after you progress to having Rover carry an uncooked egg! If you're using hard-boiled eggs, you can have your dog help with the Easter egg hunt. Maybe you can even teach him to be your partner in an egg-toss contest!

⊙ **HAND SIGNAL**
ℬ **VERBAL CUE:** "Carry the egg"
✿ **TOOLS:** Praise
⏱ **AVG. TIME:** 7-10 Days
➕ **DIFFICULTY:** Advanced

STEP-BY-STEP

1. Begin with a hard-boiled egg. Tell Rover, "Take it" (sidebar page 45).

2. While he is holding it, gently stroke him under the chin and tell him, "Good dog, good dog."

3. Let him hold the egg for a short period. Put your hand out and tell him, "Drop it" (page 13). Give him lots of praise.

Begin with a hard-boiled egg. Tell Rover, "Take it" (sidebar page 45).

4. Once he's good at holding the egg, skip the praise. Begin to walk with him. Say, "Carry the egg" as you walk with him. Have him Drop It when you're done.

5. Practice building up the length of time that he carries the egg. Once he can carry the egg and give it back to you without any cracks, move to a soft-boiled egg. Repeat the same steps, and then go through the same steps with an uncooked egg.

6. Practice three to five times a day for seven to ten days.

Let him hold the egg for a short period. Put your hand out and tell him, "Drop it" (page 13). Give him lots of praise.

ADVICE FROM THE EXPERT

Be sure to use a soft voice when training this trick. If your dog is excited he might chomp down on the egg. Repetition and patience are also important.

PROBLEM SOLVING

Problem: Your dog bites down too hard on the egg, creating cracks.

Solution: Rover needs a soft, gentle mouth for this trick, and that's something you can encourage by using a gentle voice and quiet body language. Don't let him grab at it. If he's excited let him settle down before you offer the egg again.

Begin to walk with him. Say, "Carry the egg" as you walk with him. Have him Drop It when you're done.

★ BOBBING FOR APPLES ★

- ⊕ **HAND SIGNAL**
- ✌ **VERBAL CUE:** "Apple"
- ⚙ **TOOLS:** Clicker and Treats
- ⏱ **AVG. TIME:** 5-7 Days
- ✚ **DIFFICULTY:** Intermediate

This trick is sure to entertain a houseful of guests, especially in the fall or at a Halloween party. Dress Rover in his favorite costume and let him join in the fun! If your dog doesn't like water, use string to suspend apples from a clothesline. You can also transform this trick into Bobbing for Treats by putting treats in a bowl, then hiding them with dirt or sand. Imagine Rover's big grin and dirty brown face when he finds the treat!

STEP-BY-STEP

1. Start with a very shallow, small pan. Add a small amount of water; not enough for the apples to float, just enough to smell and see the water.

2. Fill the pan with wall-to-wall apples. There should be no way the apples can move when you go to get one, and several should be sitting on top of the others so the dog doesn't have to put his face in the water.

3. Bring Rover to the pan and tell him, "Take it, apple" (page 45). Once he grabs an apple, click and treat.

Show your dog the pan and tell him, "Take it, apple."

4. Return the apple to the pan and do it again. Repeat five times.

5. Next time, remove one apple from the pan and repeat the step five times.

6. With each practice session, decrease the apples by one until they're freely floating around.

7. Practice three to five times a day for several days.

Once he takes the apple be sure to click and treat.

★ ADVICE FROM THE EXPERT

Don't worry if your dog wants to eat the apple. They're a great source of calcium and vitamin C. Just make sure to core it beforehand or cut it into pieces so he can't ingest the seeds.

✦ PROBLEM SOLVING

Problem: Your dog wants to drink the water.

Solution: Do this trick without water in the bowl.

Problem: Your dog can't get a hold of the apple and loses interest.

Solution: This isn't unusual, especially if you have a small dog who can't get his whole mouth around the entire apple. Practice with an apple alone, no water. Roll it on the floor like a ball and have Rover Fetch (page 31). Reinforce the Apple command by associating the fruit with the word, and make it fun!

★ CHASE YOUR TAIL ★

This trick is hilarious to watch. Who doesn't love a dog chasing his tail! You'll need patience to turn this movement into a trick where Rover spins around and around, but the time and effort are worth the praise and hoorays! Once he's mastered the trick you can use alternative phrases or funny questions as your cue, such as, "Who's a whirling dervish?" You can also link this trick with other spinning tricks such as Pirouette (page 80).

⊕ HAND SIGNAL
VERBAL CUE: "Chase your tail"
✿ TOOLS: Clicker, Praise and Treats
⊙ AVG. TIME: 5-7 Days
✚ DIFFICULTY: Intermediate

STEP-BY-STEP

1. Place peanut butter (his reward) on Rover's tail. If he has a long tail, bring the tail to his mouth and let him taste the peanut butter.

2. Tell him, "Chase your tail" as he tries to get the peanut butter off his tail.

3. Another option: Use a treat to lure him around in a circle, as if he's chasing his tail. You want to capture the behavior as he spins, so keep saying, "Chase your tail, chase your tail."

Show your dog the treat.

4. Another option: Put a piece of masking tape on the end of his tail. It will annoy him so much that he will start chasing his tail to get off the tape. Click as he spins, telling him, "Chase your tail, chase your tail," and give him a treat.

5. Practice three to five times a day for five to seven days.

Use the treat to lure your dog around in a circle.

 ADVICE FROM THE EXPERT

If your dog has no interest in peanut butter use cream cheese or tickle the base of his tail. As he turns around to see what you're doing, say, "Chase your tail!"

PROBLEM SOLVING

Problem: Your dog doesn't catch on to the concept of spin.

Solution: If you're using a treat to lure him, hold the treat in your hand and spin it around, saying, "Chase your tail!" If you're tickling his tail, keep playing with it and using the command. He will keep circling around out of frustration, and you can click and reward!

Tell him, "Chase your tail!" as he starts to turn.

★ PEEKABOO ★

● **HAND SIGNAL**

🔊 **VERBAL CUE:** "Peekaboo"

⚙ **TOOLS:** Clicker and Treats

🕐 **AVG. TIME:** 3-5 Days

➕ **DIFFICULTY:** Beginner

Most everyone knows the childhood game of Peekaboo I see you! It's a great trick to teach your dog. Once he understands the concept of Peekaboo you can transfer the idea to any number of situations. Have your dog peek out from behind the furniture or drapes, from around a corner, under a blanket, jacket or soft pillow. You can even work up a skit with two dogs peeking in succession, set the trick music, or have a child and your dog peek at each other around another dog. The possibilities are endless!

STEP-BY-STEP

1. Place Rover under a table with a tablecloth hanging down. Tell him, "Sit-stay" (Stay, step 8, page 11).

Place Rover under a table with a tablecloth hanging down.

Tell him, "Peekaboo." If he sticks his head out looking for the treat, click and give him a treat.

2. Tell him, "Peekaboo." If he sticks his head out looking for the treat, click and give him a treat.

3. If he gets up and walks to you, lead him back under the table and say, "Sit-stay." Repeat the Peekaboo command.

4. Practice three to five times a day for three to five days. Eventually you can advance to having him peek out from under or behind other objects.

 ADVICE FROM THE EXPERT

The key here is to time your click just right. Use the clicker at the exact moment your dog sticks his face out from under the tablecloth.

PROBLEM SOLVING

Problem: Your dog peeks out, then trots out from his hiding place instead of staying put and peeking again.

Solution: Lead him back to the spot and reinforce Sit-stay (Stay, step 8, page 11). If he still doesn't catch on go back to basics and be sure he's mastered Sit-stay before you add Peekaboo.

Here's a fun alternative: Have your dog peek out from behind a blanket.

★ LET'S PLAY ★ BASEBALL

⊕ **HAND SIGNAL**
🐾 **VERBAL CUE:** "Swing the bat, Hit the ball, Run the bases"
⚙ **TOOLS:** Praise and Treats
🕐 **AVG. TIME:** 3-4 Weeks
✚ **DIFFICULTY:** Advanced

Baseball is the national pastime, and as American as apple pie, so let's get Rover in the game! Hand out peanuts and caps for your guests, then T-up your dog for an entertaining game of baseball. You can add in other moves or build a skit with this trick. Imagine multiple dogs! Have a few dogs take a turn at batting, then have an intermission where one dog puts on the Frisbee show. You can even toss out T-shirts for the guests (or dogs!) to catch—and don't forget the hot dogs.

This is an advanced trick. Rover needs to learn what the bat is (fairly easy), how to swing it using his head (intermediate), how to connect the swing with the ball (moderately advanced) and finally how to drop the bat and run around the bases. You and he can do it with lots of repetition, plenty of patience on your part and a strong bond between the two of you.

STEP-BY-STEP

1. This trick is best trained in two parts: Teach your dog how to bat, and teach your dog how to run the bases. Once he's mastered both pieces you can put them together for the final trick.

2. Teach your dog what the bat is using Name That Thingamajig (page 33).

3. Tell him, "Take the bat."

4. Once he's familiar with the bat and carrying it, position him in front of the T-ball stand (the batting tee) and tell him, "Sit-stay" (Stay, step 8, page 11). It will take some practice to get your dog to sit in the right location and hold the bat at the right angle. Be patient and work in baby steps if needed.

5. When he's mastered the correct positioning, have him Shake Your Head No (page 55). Say, "Shake no" and "Swing the bat." Give him lots of praise, even if he's just moving the bat slightly from one side to another. Swinging it at the right angle to knock the ball off the stand will require building muscle strength and muscle memory in his neck.

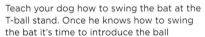
Teach your dog how to swing the bat at the T-ball stand. Once he knows how to swing the bat it's time to introduce the ball

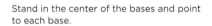
Stand in the center of the bases and point to each base.

Praise him as he touches each base in succession.

 ADVICE FROM THE EXPERT

Make sure you're using the right size plastic or foam bat for your dog. Kid-style baseball bats and T-ball stands (sometimes called batting tees) come in all sizes, from toddler to teen. You can also use a foam ball or tennis ball and broom handle cut down to the right size for a game of old-fashioned stickball or substitute a whiffle ball and bat.

PROBLEM SOLVING

Problem: Your dog isn't catching on.

Solution: Although every dog can learn this trick, make no bones about it, this is an advanced trick with several complex movements. Don't try to teach the entire swing, hit and score a home run all at once, especially if you have a dog that easily gets bored or has low endurance. Start with the swing and perfect the move. Give lots of praise. Then add the hitting and give lots of praise. Eventually you can add the base running, one base at a time. Pay close attention to your dog's body language. If he's disengaged or getting frustrated take a break and go back to it later.

6. Introduce the ball. Place it on the T-ball stand and tell him, "Swing the bat, Hit the ball." Be patient and use lots of praise. Demonstrate what you're looking for if he doesn't seem to catch on.

7. When he hits the ball, tell him, "Drop it" (page 13) so he releases the bat before he starts running the bases.

8. Set up the bases in a rough diamond pattern. Walk your dog around the bases and say, "Touch it" (page 22) for each base.

9. Run the bases with your dog, luring him along using a treat. Make sure you say, "Touch it" as you cross each base. When you get to home base give him a treat and lots of praise.

10. Stand in the center of the bases and point to each base as you tell him, "Touch it, run the bases." Praise him as he touches each base.

11. Last but not least, put the two pieces of the trick (hitting and running) together for a complete home run!

12. Practice three to five times a day for three to four weeks.

★ LET'S PLAY ★ BASKETBALL

○ **HAND SIGNAL**
🅑 **VERBAL CUE:** "Play basketball"
⚙ **TOOLS:** Praise and Treats
🕐 **AVG. TIME:** 7-10 Days
✚ **DIFFICULTY:** Advanced

Whether you're an NBA fan or you prefer college hoop, basketball is a fast-moving and exciting game, the perfect place for Rover to put on a show! There are three basic moves here: get the ball, paws up on the hoop and make the dunk shot. It's easy to play with this concept to make your own tricks. You can teach Rover to pick up an ice cube, put his paws up on a chair and drop the ice cube in a glass on the table. Have your miniature dog pick up a balled up piece of paper and drop it in the wastebasket.

STEP-BY-STEP

1. Get a foam basketball. Teach your dog what the basketball is using Name That Thingamajig (page 33).

2. Practice Take It (page 45) and Drop It (page 13) with the basketball.

3. Tell him, "Paws up" (sidebar page 19) and point to the basketball hoop. If he can't make it all the way up, stand next to the hoop and tell him, "Paws up" on your knee. Give him a treat and lots of praise.

Teach your dog Paws Up on the basketball hoop

Tell him, "Take it" with the basketball.

After he has the ball in his mouth, use the command Paws Up on the basketball hoop again.

Last but not least, have him dunk it.

 ADVICE FROM THE EXPERT

This advanced trick is fairly quick to master. When you break it down you have three basic steps: Take It (page 45), Paws Up (page 19) and Drop It (page 13). If your dog has these three moves mastered he should be ready for full court!

PROBLEM SOLVING

Problem: Your dog's too short to reach the basketball hoop.

Solution: Make your own variation on this trick. Have him Hup (page 28) onto a chair and Paws Up (page 19) to the hoop, or just Hup onto the chair and Drop It (page 13) into the hoop.

4. Once he's mastered Paws Up in the right place, tell him, "Take it" to get the ball, "Paws up" to position the ball and "Drop it" to make the shot. It may take some practice for him to position the ball correctly to drop it through the hoop.

5. Once the dog reliably performs, add the cue "Play basketball." The string is: "Take it, paws up, drop it, play basketball." Drop cues one at a time until only "Play Basketball" remains.

6. Practice three to five times a day for seven to ten days.

★ LET'S GO BOWLING ★

⊕ **HAND SIGNAL**

ℬ **VERBAL CUE:** "Let's bowl"

✿ **TOOLS:** Clicker, Praise and Treats

⏱ **AVG. TIME:** 5-7 Days

✛ **DIFFICULTY:** Intermediate

Everybody loves bowling, whether you're playing candlepin bowling for fun or competing for a ninepin strike in a team competition. Get Rover into the fun as well. There's no need for a visit to the neighborhood bowling alley; This canine version of the game uses a kid's bowling ball set and a foam ball for safe entertainment! Who knows—Rover could end up the bowling star at the neighborhood sports extravaganza!

STEP-BY-STEP

The steps below illustrate an easier, intermediate version of Bowling. For the advanced variation, see next page.

1. Set up the pins for your dog. Place the ball about one foot/0.3 m in front of the pins.

2. Tell him, "Take it" (page 45) with the bowling ball, then, "Let's bowl." The idea is to get him to carry the ball forward in any increment, even just a few inches/centimeters. Click and reward.

Set up the pins and place the ball in front of the pins.

Tell him, "Take it" with the bowling ball.

Encourage your dog to carry the ball towards the pins.

Use the ball to knock the pins down.

3. Repeat the process, encouraging him to Take It and walk forward with the ball towards the pins. Click and reward any forward movement. If he reaches the pins and knocks even one pin down be sure to heartily praise him, click and reward.

4. As he advances, use "Let's bowl" alone. Each day you work at it, encourage him to knock more pins down.

5. Practice three to five times a day for five to seven days.

ADVANCED BOWLING

1. Set up the pins for your dog. Place the ball about one foot/0.3 m in front of the pins.

2. Give him the bowling ball and tell him, "Bump" (page 27) and "Let's bowl." Click and reward.

3. Repeat the process, encouraging him to keep Bumping the ball towards the pins. If the ball reaches the pins and knocks even one pin down be sure to praise him, click and reward.

4. As he gets more comfortable/successful, drop the "Bump" command and just use "Let's bowl" alone.

5. Once the dog understands Let's Bowl, increase the distance he needs to Bump the ball. Each day you work at it, add a little more distance and encourage him to Bump the pins harder and harder. Eventually he'll knock them all down. That's the time for a special treat!

ADVICE FROM THE EXPERT

Be wary of jumping into more advanced tricks without some basic building blocks in place. It can be done, but it will take longer and require more patience on your part for your dog to master any foundational skills required as well as the new moves associated with an advanced trick.

PROBLEM SOLVING

Problem: Your dog doesn't seem to understand using the ball to knock down the pins.

Solution: Back up a few steps and teach him to Bump (page 27) the pins without the ball. Once he understands how to Bump the pins with his nose you can reintroduce the idea of using the ball.

★ PLAY GOLF ★

- ◉ **HAND SIGNAL**
- 🐾 **VERBAL CUE:** "Play golf"
- ⚙ **TOOLS:** Clicker and Praise
- 🕐 **AVG. TIME:** 7-10 Days
- ✚ **DIFFICULTY:** Advanced

If your dog can swing a baseball bat (Let's Play Baseball, page 134) he can swing a golf club! This is a great trick to mix with creative versions of others to create a skit. Have your dog pull over the golf bag (adapt Bring Me a Bag of Leaves, page 40), then pull a club out of the bag (Get the Mail, page 48). You can hit the ball and have your dog retrieve it (Name That Thingamajig, page 33; Fetch, page 31) or let Rover have a turn sending the ball down your pretend fairway (Bump, page 27). Last but not least, set up a flag on your canine putting green and have your dog Bump or Drop (page 13) the ball into the cup!

STEP-BY-STEP

1. Teach your dog to identify the golf bag and the golf club using Name That Thingamajig (page 33).

2. Point to the club and tell him, "Take it" (page 45). If needed, hold the golf club with the head on the floor and the shaft close to his mouth. The goal is to have him hold the golf club in the right position. Use lots of praise if he does anything close to that. Repeat several times, using lots of praise or a clicker as he perfects the technique.

Point to the golf club and tell your dog, "Take it." If needed, hold the shaft of the club close to his mouth.

3. Position the ball on the ground and tell your dog, "Take it, touch it, play golf" (Touch It, page 22). The goal here is to get him comfortable with the club in the right position (step 2) and with his paw on the club. This will take time and practice. Use lots of praise.

4. Show him how you want him to move the club with his paw and say, "Play golf." This will take time, patience and lots of praise.

Use lots of praise when he takes the club.

Show him how you want him to move the club with his paw.

 ADVICE FROM THE EXPERT

It may sound obvious, but make sure you use a kid-size plastic or foam golf set for this trick. Both materials will allow Rover to get a good grip on the club.

PROBLEM SOLVING

Problem: Your dog takes the club but holds it horizontally in his mouth, like he would hold a stick.

Solution: He needs to hold the club with the end in his mouth to successfully swing the club. You can practice this by using a baton or a stick with a very blunt end. Use a treat and praise or the clicker as he learns the correct position.

★ CONGA LINE ★

⊕ **HAND SIGNAL**
✎ **VERBAL CUE:** "Let's conga!"
⚙ **TOOLS:** Praise and Treats
🕐 **AVG. TIME:** 7-10 Days
➕ **DIFFICULTY:** Advanced

If you've been to a wedding or bar mitzvah, you're probably familiar with the conga line, a dance that originated in Cuba. Participants form a long line with their hands on the back or waist of the person preceding them, and the dancers make three shuffling steps followed by a small kick. It's a fun and entertaining group dance that moves around an entire room, and now Rover can join right in (minus the last little kick)! Once your dog has mastered Conga Line you can introduce conga music and use that as the cue!

STEP-BY-STEP

1. Place your back to your dog and tell Rover, "Paws up" (sidebar page 19). Alternatively, use a helper and have your dog do Paws Up on that person. Depending on the height of you/your helper the dog's paws may be on your/his shoulders or back. Either position is fine. Give Rover a treat and plenty of praise.

2. Take one very small step forward. Tell Rover, "Let's conga!" After he moves with you, stop and give him praise.

3. Take two very small steps forward. Tell Rover, "Let's conga!" After he moves with you, stop and give him praise.

4. Repeat, each time taking an additional very small step forward.

5. Practice this several times a day for about a week. For the advanced version add in conga music for the cue.

ADVICE FROM THE EXPERT
There are two essential parts to this trick. First, your dog should have Paws Up (page 19) down pat. Second, when you or your helper starts walking forward, you should move very slowly, one small step at a time. If you move too quickly your dog will come down.

🦴 PROBLEM SOLVING
Problem: Your dog can handle Paws Up but doesn't stay up long enough to learn the dance.

Solution: Practice Paws Up for fifteen seconds, then thirty seconds, then forty-five and sixty, and so on. Rover needs to get used to standing on his hind legs and develop the muscle strength to hold himself up.

★ SIT PRETTY ★
ON MY BACK

Here's a slightly more advanced version of Pony Ride (page 146). You can make a great skit using a string of tricks that include you: Jump Over Me (page 102), Pony Ride (page 146), Jump through My Arms (page 168), or Jump over My Leg (page 166), even Scratch my Back (page 163).

⊕ HAND SIGNAL
✍ VERBAL CUE: "Sit high"
✿ TOOLS: Praise
⏱ AVG. TIME: 7-10 Days
✛ DIFFICULTY: Advanced

STEP-BY-STEP

1. Teach your dog Pony Ride (page 146) and Sit Pretty (page 18). He needs to have mastered both these tricks separately before you can put them together. Use a helper if needed.

2. Tell him, "Jump on my back" and "Sit-stay" (page 11). Use lots of praise as he completes these two cues together.

3. Once he's on your back consistently, tell him, "Sit pretty." Repeat several times using lots of praise.

4. Tell him, "Jump on my back" and "Sit pretty." Voilà!

5. Practice three to five times a day for seven to ten days.

 ADVICE FROM THE EXPERT

It's worth revisiting foundational moves from time to time to make sure your dog remembers them and consistently completes them with a verbal cue. This trick is a good time for revisiting Sit-stay (page 11) and even Down-stay (page 14).

★ STRUM A GUITAR ★

⊕ HAND SIGNAL
✋ VERBAL CUE: "Strum"
⚙ TOOLS: Clicker and Treats
⏱ AVG. TIME: 5-7 Days
✚ DIFFICULTY: Intermediate

We all know Rover's not likely to be the next Paul McCartney, Jimmy Page or B.B. King, but that doesn't mean he can't learn to strum a guitar and even have a canine or human companion sing along! As with all tricks that involve a level of refinement, be consistent and patient. With time Rover will be strumming his version of "Dog Days Are Over," "Hound Dog" or "Who Let the Dogs Out?"

The key word here is strum, which is a gentle version of your dog pawing at something. For some dogs this action will come naturally, while for others it will take more time and practice. Start out with a inexpensive kid's guitar—a yard sale find is best—and make sure Rover's nails are clipped to reduce the number of scratches.

STEP-BY-STEP

1. Position the guitar on the floor with the strings facing up.

Position the guitar on the floor with the strings facing up.

Tell him, "Paws up" (sidebar page 19). As soon as he touches it, even tentatively, click and reward.

2. Place Rover in front of the guitar. Tell him, "Paws up" (sidebar page 19). As soon as he touches it, even tentatively, click and reward. Repeat the process, using Paws Up.

3. Point to the strings on the guitar and say, "Touch it" (page 22). Click and reward any placement of the paws near the strings.

4. Strum the strings to show him it makes noise. Hold the guitar in one hand and his paw in the other and demonstrate how his pawing will also make noise. Stay, "Strum."

5. Each time you practice, encourage him to position his paws on the string. The more he touches it, the more sound he will get. Every time he makes a sound, say, "Strum." As the sound increases and the treats increase, he will hit it more and more.

6. Practice three to five times a day for five to seven days.

Each time you practice, encourage him to position his paws on the string.

 ADVICE FROM THE EXPERT

I recommend using treats rather than clicks when teaching Strum a Guitar, especially when you've got one hand on his paw and the other on the guitar. It's too complicated to add a click in there, so use a small treat instead.

PROBLEM SOLVING

Problem: Your dog paws at the strings too roughly and/or the pawing action doesn't produce music.

Solution: Slow it down, sit next to him and gently manipulate his paw with your hand. Say, "strum" over and over as you show him the movement.

★ PONY RIDE ★

This simple version of the grown-up circus trick—having a dog ride on the back of a moving pony—is a fun and entertaining trick for little dogs. It's also fun to get the kids involved. Once Rover has mastered this move, you can string it together with assorted tricks that involve you or a helper and your dog moving together. If you've got a tiny dog (eight pounds/3.6 kg and under) and a big dog (e.g., Bernese Mountain Dog or Newfoundland), you can teach the smaller dog to ride on the back of the big dog!

⊕ **HAND SIGNAL**
🖐 **VERBAL CUE:** "Ride on my back"
⚙ **TOOLS:** Praise and Treats
⏱ **AVG. TIME:** 5-7 Days
✚ **DIFFICULTY:** Advanced

STEP-BY-STEP

1. Get down on all fours. Have your assistant point to your back. Tell your dog, "Paws up" (sidebar page 19).

2. Once he's mastered Paws Up to your back, use Hup (page 28) to get him on your back. Have your helper spot him to prevent him from over-jumping.

Tell your dog, "Paws up" onto your back.

Tell your dog, "Hup" onto your back. Have your helper point to your back.

3. If he's a medium-sized dog, tell him to Sit-stay (Stay, step 8, page 11). If he's a little dog, tell him to Stand-stay (Stay, step 9, page 11). Let him practice this a few times so he gets used to standing on your back before you start crawling. Give him a treat and praise him after he's done.

4. When you're ready to advance, take one small crawling movement at a time. Have your assistant gauge the dog's reaction. If he seems fine, keep crawling! Again, have your assistant serve as spotter so Rover doesn't fall. Offer a treat and praise.

5. Work up to crawling around in a small circle. Practice several times a day for five to seven days before you try having Rover jump onto anyone else's back.

Once he's comfortable standing you can crawl forward.

Alternatively, have your dog Down-Stay while you crawl.

 ADVICE FROM THE EXPERT

Although you can teach this trick with medium-sized dogs, be careful if you have back problems. Be sure to have a helper to point to your back as you issue commands.

PROBLEM SOLVING

Problem: Your dog understands Hup (page 28) and jumps up on your back but then immediately jumps down.

Solution: You need a firm voice, especially since you can't look him in the eye, and assistance from your helper. Once he's up, tell him Sit-stay and Stand-stay and have your helper hold him by the collar. Praise him while your assistant hands him a little treat. Start out with a fifteen-second stay, then move up to thirty seconds, forty-five seconds, and so on while you praise him repeatedly. Alternatively, use Down-Stay (Down, step 5, page 14) and let him sit while he rides.

★ PLAY HORSESHOES ★

⊕ HAND SIGNAL
☝ VERBAL CUE: "Play horseshoes"
✿ TOOLS: Praise
⊙ AVG. TIME: 7-10 Days
✛ DIFFICULTY: Advanced

You'd never play real horseshoes with your dog, but you can adopt this classic game for a fun and entertaining canine version! Instead of metal horseshoes use soft foam rings, and instead of a horseshoe stake you'll use Rover! Have fun with this trick. You can train two dogs and alternate throwing them onto each dog, or teach Rover to trot back over to you and drop his head to return the rings.

STEP-BY-STEP

1. Perfect your ring toss. Practice on an object about the size of your dog.

2. Show your dog the rings. Let him sniff them and see they're nothing to be afraid of. Tell him, "Sit-stay" (page 11). Hold strong eye-to-eye contact with him.

Hold the rings in your hand. Put your dog in a Sit-stay.

Maintain eye-to-eye contact as you toss the ring.

Praise your dog after you've tossed one ring around his neck.

Toss the second ring to complete your trick!

 ADVICE FROM THE EXPERT

The first and most important step in training this trick is for you to master throwing the rings around a stationary object. You've got to perfect your throw as much as possible before you involve your dog. You don't want to hit Rover in the face with the ring!

3. Slowly toss the ring around his neck and use the command, "Play horseshoes." Praise him. Toss the second ring around his neck. Tell him, "Good dog, good play horseshoes!"

4. Practice three to five times a day for seven to ten days.

PROBLEM SOLVING

Problem: Your dog shies away, ducks his head or turns to the side as you toss the rings.

Solution: Back up a few steps in your training and start over. Show him the rings so he's comfortable. Put one around his neck and let him wear it for awhile. Spend time putting it on and taking it off. Slowly transition to tossing it. If you're at all unsure of your ability, use soft foam or even fabric rings.

FOR A VARATION

Teach your dog to catch the rings as you toss them—similar to Catch a Frisbee (page 44).

★ PUSH A SKATEBOARD ★

⊕ **HAND SIGNAL**
✌ **VERBAL CUE:** "Push the skateboard"
⚙ **TOOLS:** Clicker, Treats and Praise
🕐 **AVG. TIME:** 3-4 Weeks
✚ **DIFFICULTY:** Advanced

This is one of those tricks that makes a great television commercial: the skateboarding dog. This safe version will entertain the whole neighborhood, especially if you ham it up and dress Rover with a bandana or other skateboard gear. Once he's mastered this, you can add other elements. Teach him to push the skateboard around a set of cones, jump over the skateboard or even get a second dog involved!

STEP-BY-STEP

1. Introduce the skateboard to your dog. Let him sniff it and paw at it. Show him that it moves.

2. Tell him, "Paws up" (sidebar page 19) while pointing to the skateboard. Pat the skateboard if he's unsure what you mean, and hold onto the board if he seems nervous. Give him lots of praise even if he touches it and then backs off.

Tell your dog, "Paws up" on the skateboard.

Tell him, "Touch it" and point to the skateboard.

Stay along side your dog as he learns to push the board.

2. Once he's mastered Paws Up, you can introduce the idea of pushing the skateboard. This will take some time and patience. Show him that it moves and use the cue, "Push."

3. Go very slowly and move the board for him one to two inches/2.5 to 5.1 cm at first, saying, "Push."

4. When he's comfortable with this initial action you can encourage him to push it along further. Again, keep your hand on the board to prevent it from sliding out from under him.

5. Eventually you can transition to using the cue "push the skateboard" and let him move it on his own.

 ADVICE FROM THE EXPERT

Your dog should be comfortable with movement in order to succeed at this trick. For example, if he's good at Roll a Barrel (page 86), he should take to this trick easily.

PROBLEM SOLVING

Problem: Your dog doesn't catch on to the push action.

Solution: Teach your dog Paws Up (sidebar page 19) on the board. This alone may be your trick, or you can show him how to push it sideways from this position. That's a little more challenging in some ways but certain dogs will find it easier.

★ CHAPTER SEVEN ★

SHOW OFF

Ready for the big time? Want to land Rover on the doggie version of "America's Got Talent?" Here's a whole set of tricks that can put you in the big leagues, whether you're trying to take Rover to Hollywood or just creating your own canine performance!

Many of the tricks in this chapter are action-oriented and best suited for athletic and well-coordinated dogs. You're sure to blow away your guests when Rover Climbs a Ladder (page 158) and then Jumps through a Closed Hoop (page 160) just like a circus dog!

I've also gathered a few tricks that are just fun—Drive a Car (page 155), Scratch My Back (page 163), Go Hide (page 170) and Refuse Food (page 162). Whatever tricks you choose, it's all about creating (and tapping into) a close bond between you and your dog. Now let's hit the field and get ready for fun and games!

★ TELL ME A SECRET ★

Shhhhhh—I've got a secret to tell you! Here's a fun and fairly easy trick to teach your dog. It's a great move for involving kids or other participants. They'll get a kick out of training your dog too, because they get to put a little dab of peanut butter on their ear.

⊕ HAND SIGNAL
✋ VERBAL CUE: "Tell me a secret"
⚙ TOOLS: Treats
⊙ AVG. TIME: 3-5 Days
✚ DIFFICULTY: Beginner

STEP-BY-STEP

1. This trick is identical to Kiss (page 64), but you place a tiny amount of peanut butter or cream cheese on your ear instead of your cheek.

2. Tap your ear and say, "Tell me a secret."

3. Practice three to five times a day for three to five days, eventually removing the food incentive and giving him lots of praise when he licks your ear.

🎖 ADVICE FROM THE EXPERT
Although it may sound like a good idea, don't use a hard dog treat with this trick. The treat could get stuck in your ear.

🦴 PROBLEM SOLVING
Problem: Your dog licks at the peanut butter, so it doesn't look like he's telling a secret.
Solution: Use only a tiny dab so he doesn't need his entire tongue.

READ A BOOK ★

★ HAND SIGNAL
🐾 VERBAL CUE: "Read"
⚙ TOOLS: Praise and Treats
🕐 AVG. TIME: 3-5 Days
➕ DIFFICULTY: Beginner

Rover's not only smart, he's book smart! I love this trick. It's always funny to see a dog taking on a quintessentially human action, and this is an easy one for Rover to master.

STEP-BY-STEP

1. Start with a lightweight, oversized children's book.

2. Tell your dog, "Down" (page 14). Open the book and lay it flat in front of him. Put a treat in the space between the pages, along the spine. Tell him, "Touch it" (page 22) and "read." Let him take the treat, then give him praise.

3. Repeat five times, then place treats in between a few pages. Tell him, "Touch it" and "read" and let him find the treats. Transition to using the Read command alone.

3. After practicing for three to five days, start to wean him off the treats and use lots of praise as the reward.

 ADVICE FROM THE EXPERT

Cut back on the treats if your dog gets really excited about food or starts scratching at the pages. This is a trick that requires a calm, focused dog. It will be difficult to teach if he's amped up, so discourage that by using quiet body language and a calm tone of voice.

PROBLEM SOLVING

Problem: Your dog won't stay down after he finds the treat. He jumps up and starts hunting for more food.

Solution: There are two problems here. One, he needs a solid, steady Down (page 14) for success, and may need to review. Second, try using the clicker or just praise as the reward.

★ DRIVE A CAR ★

⊕ HAND SIGNAL
✋ VERBAL CUE: "Drive"
✿ TOOLS: Praise and Treats
⏱ AVG. TIME: 1-2 Weeks
✚ DIFFICULTY: Intermediate

I love this trick, especially the effect it creates with a group of two to three small dogs sitting together in a miniature kid's car. If you can get the driver to wear sunglasses and the dog who's got shotgun to wear a scarf tied under her throat you can create your own version of old-time Hollywood stars Clark Gable and Grace Kelly. Outfit the driver with a gangster hat and the dog in the front passenger seat with a beret and you've got a canine version of the famous outlaws Bonnie and Clyde!

STEP-BY-STEP

1. Tell your dog, "Hup" (page 28) to get him to jump into the driver's seat. Use lots of praise.

2. Once he's mastered jumping into the car, tell him, "Paws up, drive" (Paws up, sidebar page 19), with the goal being the dog's paws on the steering wheel. Then tell him, "Stay" (page 11). Give him a treat and lots of praise.

4. Repeat using all four commands: "Hup, Paws Up, Drive, Stay." Eventually drop Stay, followed by Paws Up, and lastly Hup. Your goal is to transition to just using the command Drive.

5. Practice three to four times per day for one to two weeks.

🏅 ADVICE FROM THE EXPERT

Start your training by introducing the car and making sure your dog is comfortable going into a small space, especially if you're using a closed car, not a convertible.

🦴 PROBLEM SOLVING

Problem: Your dog will get into the car, but looks uncomfortable and jumps right out.

Solution: Move away from the car for a few days and reinforce Stay (page 11) and Paws Up (page 19). Let him transition back to the trick by getting familiar with the car. Let him sniff it, Paws Up on the outside, and so on. Eventually you can move to having him Hup into the car and having him Sit on the seat. Once he's comfortable doing this consistently, introduce Paws Up on the steering wheel.

★ JUMP THROUGH ★ A HOOP

You can have a lot of fun with this trick. From this basic move you can advance to having your dog perform Jump through a Closed Hoop (page 160) or Jump through My Arms (page 168). The most advanced version of this trick that I know, jumping through a flaming hoop, isn't for anyone but serious dog-training professionals, but simpler variations can be just as entertaining!

⊕ HAND SIGNAL
✌ VERBAL CUE: "Hup"
✿ TOOLS: Praise and Treats
⊙ AVG. TIME: 7-10 Days
✚ DIFFICULTY: Intermediate

STEP-BY-STEP

1. You'll need a plastic hoop such as a Hula-Hoop or a large embroidery hoop from a craft store.

2. Place your dog in a Sit-stay (Stay, step 8, page 11) on your side.

Start with your dog in a Sit-stay.

3. Stand the hoop in front of him with your outside hand. Hold a treat in your right hand on the other side of the hoop. Tell him, "Hup" (page 28). As he walks/jumps through the hoop, give him lots of praise. With your hand holding the treat, lure him behind you and give him the treat. It's okay to get him excited here!

4. Repeat five to eight times the first session.

5. Practice three to four times a day, each time bringing the hoop up a little bit higher until he actually has to Hup to get through it.

6. Practice two to three times a day for seven to ten days.

Once you've lured him through the hoop with a treat a few times, he'll start to do it on his own.

ADVICE FROM THE EXPERT

I have one critical piece of advice when teaching this trick: Don't let your dog go around or under the hoop, not even once. If he figures out an escape route it will be very difficult to get him to go through the hoop.

🦴 PROBLEM SOLVING

Problem: Oops! Your dog found a way under or around the hoop.

Solution: Take a break from training the trick and let Rover go play. This will clear his mind and increase your odds that he won't remember how to escape. Once you return to the training use a helper if needed. You may have to move the hoop in order to put your dog through it, rather than having him go through it on his own, to get the treat. It can also help to train him in a narrow hallway where he can't go around the hoop.

★ CLIMB A LADDER ★

Here's another trick straight from the agility competition! This advanced move requires excellent body balancing and a fearless attitude, engendered in part because you'll be there to spot him and he trusts you. It's easiest for small dogs, but most dogs can learn this trick given time and patience.

⊕ **HAND SIGNAL**
✋ **VERBAL CUE:** "Climb"
⚙ **TOOLS:** Praise and Treats
🕐 **AVG. TIME:** 7-10 Days
✚ **DIFFICULTY:** Advanced

STEP-BY-STEP

1. You'll need a sturdy ladder with five steps for this trick. Start by covering the steps with a nonslip surface. You need very good traction to keep your dog safe.

2. Hold the ladder steady with one hand. Tell your dog, "Paws up" (sidebar page 19) and use a treat to lure him to put his paws on the second or third rung of the ladder (depending on his height). Repeat several times and only for three to five minutes total.

Tell your dog, "Paws up" to get his front feet on the ladder.

Say, "Climb" and use a treat to lure one of his back feet onto the lowest rung.

Suppot your dog carefully as you help him bring his second back foot onto the lowest rung.

Stay very close to your dog as he moves up the ladder.

 ADVICE FROM THE EXPERT

Take this trick very slowly. Your dog needs to be agile, strong, coordinated and confident. A misstep can be frightening and set you back. Really pause between sessions and progression up the rungs.

PROBLEM SOLVING

Problem: Your dog got scared partway up the ladder and froze.

Solution: Take him or help him off the ladder. If he seems okay, try the trick again. If not, take a break and let him go play. This will help clear his mind. Do not coddle or comfort him excessively after you bring him down, as this will reinforce the fear.

3. When he seems ready, hold the ladder steady with one hand and lure him with your other hand while you lift one of his back paws up onto the lowest rung. Use the command, "Climb." Make sure you guard his body with your hand to prevent him from falling. Again, repeat several times but only for three to five minutes total.

4. When he's ready to advance help him bring both back paws up to the lowest rung, again luring him with a treat, guarding his body with your free hand, and using the Climb command.

5. Once he gets the hang of it, place a treat at the top step to have him climb by himself. Stay close. To get him down, take each foot and teach him to walk down backwards, one foot, one step at a time. Stand behind him to prevent him from jumping or falling off.

6. Practice two or three times a day for seven to ten days, always taking care to spot him as he's learning.

JUMP THROUGH ★ A CLOSED HOOP

This is a souped-up version of Jump through a Hoop (page 156). Instead of a basic hoop, you dress up your circular prop with paper streamers and tissue paper. This can create a pretty dramatic effect. Imagine Rover bursting through a paper screen and onto your performance stage!

○ **HAND SIGNAL**
🖑 **VERBAL CUE:** "Hup"
⚙ **TOOLS:** Praise
🕐 **AVG. TIME:** 1-2 Weeks
✚ **DIFFICULTY:** Advanced

STEP-BY-STEP

1. Prepare the ring by attaching five paper streamers so they hang over the opening of the hoop. Introduce Rover to the new hoop and ask him to Hup (page 28). Give him lots of praise.

2. Add five more streamers and repeat. Give him lots of praise.

3. Once he is confident jumping through the streamers, remove the streamers and place tissue paper across the bottom half of the hoop. Make a vertical slit down the middle so he gets the feeling of breaking through the paper without getting stuck. Have him Hup through. Repeat until he is confident breaking through the bottom half.

4. Place tissue paper across the top half and the bottom half. Cut a half moon in the top tissue paper so he can see through to the other side. Have him Hup through. Once he becomes adept at this, replace the tissue paper on the top and the bottom and cut vertical slits; he will be able to jump through but not see the other side.

5. Practice each progression three to five times for three to four days before moving on to the next.

 ADVICE FROM THE EXPERT
Go slowly here, and cut bigger holes in the tissue paper if Rover appears hesitant.

PROBLEM SOLVING

Problem: Your dog won't go through the hoop.

Solution: If Rover already knows Jump through a Hoop (page 156) and does it consistently, put his leash on and gently pull him through the hoop. Once he's overcome his fear of what's behind the screen he should be fine.

★ FAKE LIMP ★

This funny trick works well in a military-themed skit. You can also get creative with your voice commands for this move. Try something like, "Rover, did you stub your toe?" or "I see the nail polish on that foot isn't dry yet?"

⊕ **HAND SIGNAL**
🔖 **VERBAL CUE:** "Limp"
⚙ **TOOLS:** Praise
🕐 **AVG. TIME:** 5-7 Days
✚ **DIFFICULTY:** Intermediate

STEP-BY-STEP

Your dog will respond better on one side than the other with this trick. The key is finding out which side is right for him. Start by working on one side, then move to the other to assess which is more comfortable for him.

1. Loop your leash under your dog's wrist while facing him. Start walking backwards and say, "Come, limp" (Come, page 12). Holding the leash up makes it impossible for him to walk without his paw lifted. Walk backwards a few steps then repeat on the other side.

2. After trying on both sides, you will be able to see which side is more comfortable for him. Put the leash under the wrist on that side to raise it up again, face your dog and walk backwards. Praise him even if he only walks one or two steps forward.

3. Continue using, "Come, limp" as the command until he walks forward four or five steps, then transition to using the Limp command alone.

4. Practice three to five times a day for five to seven days.

 ADVICE FROM THE EXPERT

The key to this trick is balance. Make sure Rover can balance on three feet comfortably before you introduce the concept of moving forward.

🦴 **PROBLEM SOLVING**

Problem: Your dog can balance on three feet but doesn't seem to grasp the concept of limping forward.

Solution: Move slowly. Although this is, on occasion, a familiar movement for a dog, it's not associated with pleasure, so you may have to overcome that mindset.

★ REFUSE FOOD ★

- ⊕ **HAND SIGNAL**
- ߷ **VERBAL CUE:** "No"
- ⚙ **TOOLS:** Praise
- ⏱ **AVG. TIME:** 5-7 Days
- ✚ **DIFFICULTY:** Beginner

Here's an entertaining trick with lots of room for creative prompting! Try linking the move to a cue such as, "Rover, you don't like liver?" or "I see you prefer your chicken grilled, not crispy?" This is also a move that can save your dog's life. If you notice him going to eat grapes or chocolate, for example, you can quickly stop him verbally. It will also teach him not to accept food from strangers.

STEP-BY-STEP

1. Enlist the help of an assistant whom your dog doesn't know. Place your dog in a Sit-stay (Stay, step 8, page 11) next to you.

2. Have your assistant offer him food. Tell him, "No!" in a deep and sharp tone. If he doesn't take it, offer him lots of praise.

3. Repeat five times the first session, always offering lots of praise.

4. Once your dog has mastered refusing food from a stranger, you can progress to having him refuse food from someone he knows. Then transition to having him refuse food that you offer. The ultimate goal is to get him to turn away from food that's offered by anyone, including you, when you issue the command.

5. Practice three to five times for five to seven days until your dog has mastered the trick.

🏅 ADVICE FROM THE EXPERT
You'll need a second person to teach this trick, and it must be someone the dog has never met before. This is key, because you don't want there to be any association between your dog and the person who offers them food.

🦴 PROBLEM SOLVING
Problem: Your dog is completely motivated by food.

Solution: Be very patient and go very slowly when training this trick. Your dog is hardwired to go for food and you're trying to rework this wiring. It can be done, but for a dog who's really interested in food it will take more time.

★ SCRATCH MY BACK ★

Here's a trick that I invented. It works great in a skit that involves your dog jumping over you: He can stop and scratch your back. Or have fun with a doggie spa day or personal assistant theme. Train your dog to bring you your hairbrush, slippers and robe (Name that Thingamajig, page 33; Fetch, page 31). Then lay on your stomach as if you're ready for a massage and have him bring you a pillow followed by a massaging Scratch My Back.

⊕ HAND SIGNAL
✌ VERBAL CUE: "Scratch my back"
✿ TOOLS: Praise
◷ AVG. TIME: 5-7 Days
✚ DIFFICULTY: Intermediate

STEP-BY-STEP

1. You will need an assistant. Sit on the floor and have your dog sit behind you.

2. Tell him, "Paws up" (sidebar page 19) onto your back. Have your assistant point to your back if needed.

3. Have your assistant move the dog's paws in a scratching motion while you tell the dog, "Scratch my back."

4. Another option: Lie flat on your stomach. Have the dog stand on your back using Hup (page 28) and tell him, "Scratch my back." Again, have your assistant mimic the action for him if needed. Praise him when he begins to scratch on his own.

5. Practice three to five times a day for five to seven days.

 ADVICE FROM THE EXPERT
Make sure your dog's nails aren't too long or too sharp before you teach this trick.

▰● PROBLEM SOLVING
Problem: Your dog doesn't keep his paws up long enough to make a scratching motion.

Solution: Teach Rover to scratch your foot, arm or leg, then transition to your back. Don't use the Dig command here. That's an action that won't feel good!

★ BALANCE AND CATCH ★

● **HAND SIGNAL**
🖐 **VERBAL CUE:** "Wait, Catch"
⚙ **TOOLS:** Praise and Treats
🕐 **AVG. TIME:** 3-4 Weeks
＋ **DIFFICULTY:** Advanced

Here's a really fun trick that impresses people every time. Your dog can learn to flip an item off his nose and catch it! This is an amazing demonstration of your dog's calm, steady focus as well as the tight bond between you and him. He needs to know you're the boss in order to wait for his treat, and especially one he can smell atop his nose!

For advanced versions of this trick, you can teach him to balance, flip and catch a small foam ball or a favorite toy. If he's ready for center stage, try teaching him to balance, flip and catch a hard-boiled egg: That requires a soft mouth as well as coordination!

STEP-BY-STEP

1. Gently hold your dog's muzzle and place a treat on his nose. Tell him, "Stay."

Hold your dog's muzzle as you put the treat on his nose.

Tell him "stay" as you slowly move your hands away.

Build up to having him wait for thirty to forty-five seconds before he can move.

2. After a few seconds, release his muzzle and slowly move your hands away. If he's really excited the treat will probably get thrown off and fall on the floor. If this happens, pretend to race him to the treat. This will motivate him to catch it himself.

3. Advance to having your dog balance the treat on his nose for up to fifteen seconds before he flips it off. Use the Stay command to build up the time. Progress to thirty seconds, then forty-five, and so on. Don't go so long you torture him—keep it fun!

4. Once he can do this consistently, you can introduce the "Catch" cue as he flips it off. It may take a lot of time and patience to teach him to catch the treat, but practice makes perfect.

5. Practice three to five times a day for three to four weeks.

 ADVICE FROM THE EXPERT

Although it seems like the balance/wait portion of this trick is the most difficult to teach, it's actually the coordination required to catch the treat as it flips off his nose that will take the most time and patience to master.

PROBLEM SOLVING

Problem: Rover's having trouble keeping his muzzle still.

Solution: Use your hand to very gently hold his muzzle in place while you cue, "Stay, stay." Keep your body language and voice very calm and quiet. Your dog has to learn how to be very still, and this requires focus on his part. If he still can't master it, try teaching it at night, when he's tired, or use another trick to relax him before the training session.

★ JUMP OVER MY LEG ★

I love all jumping tricks. I think the visual of dogs leaping is so entertaining just in itself! This is an easy one for most dogs to learn, and it works great in combination with other jumping moves such as Jump over Me (page 102) and Jump through a Hoop (page 156). For dogs who have mastered this combination, create an advanced jumping skit by adding in anything from Jump through My Arms (page 168) to Jump over Another Dog (page 94).

◉ **HAND SIGNAL**
🖑 **VERBAL CUE:** "Hup"
⚙ **TOOLS:** Praise and Treats
⏱ **AVG. TIME:** 5-7 Days
➕ **DIFFICULTY:** Intermediate

STEP-BY-STEP

1. Start about two or three feet/0.6 to 0.9 m away from a wall. Kneel on your left leg and straighten out your right leg to reach the wall.

Hold a treat in your right hand and lure him over your leg.

2. Hold a treat in your right hand, then lure Rover over your leg and use the command Hup (page 28). Give him the treat and plenty of praise.

3. Repeat several times a day for five to seven days.

4. Once he's mastered the trick by jumping between you and the wall, you can move away and practice the trick with no boundaries.

 ADVICE FROM THE EXPERT

Make sure your dog knows Hup (page 28) and adjust your knee and/or leg to match the height he's capable of clearing.

PROBLEM SOLVING

Problem: Your dog doesn't want to jump over your leg.

Solution: You can always back this up and teach your dog to "Hup" over a low object by going over the jump with him! Just put him on the leash, use a happy voice and lead him right over the jump. Don't forget the verbal cue! Try the leg again after he's reliably jumping over other objects.

Give him lots of encouragement and use the Hup command.

JUMP THROUGH MY ARMS

This is a great trick for the little guys. Although jumping through any kind of hoop is dramatic and entertaining, this one is personal! For a bigger dog work with an assistant to make a circle with both sets of arms! Your dog should be consistently Jumping through a hoop (page 156) with just a verbal cue to learn this trick.

⊕ **HAND SIGNAL**
✋ **VERBAL CUE:** "Hup"
⚙ **TOOLS:** Praise
🕐 **AVG. TIME:** 3-5 Days
➕ **DIFFICULTY:** Advanced

STEP-BY-STEP

1. Practice making a ring with your arms.

First, practice making a ring with your arms.

Have your dog practice jumping through a hoop.

2. Have your dog practice jumping through a hoop, using the Hup command (Jump through a Hoop, page 156; Hup, page 28).

3. Place your arms around the hoop and say, "Hup." Practice this several times. If you have a large dog and you're using a large hoop, your hands won't connect, but that's okay.

4. Remove the hoop, hold your arms up in a circle and say, "Hup." Be patient with this trick. He may need to get used to jumping so close to you.

5. Practice three to five times a day for three to five days.

 ADVICE FROM THE EXPERT

Be sure to adjust the size of your arm circle to match your dog's jumping ability.

PROBLEM SOLVING

Problem: your dog hesitates when it comes to jumping through your arms.

Solution: Sometimes it's confusing for a dog to move from jumping through a hoop, with you giving commands, to jumping through your arms, which is very close to you. Get a helper involved; this way you can issue the commands and lure your dog through with a treat if needed.

Have your dog jump through your arms.

★ GO HIDE ★

HAND SIGNAL
VERBAL CUE: "Go hide"
TOOLS: Praise and Treats
AVG. TIME: 5-7 Days
DIFFICULTY: Intermediate

I love combining this trick with Peekaboo (page 32)! If you've got little kids around, you can stitch together a skit that involves your dog and the kids. Have them play a game of hide-and-seek combined with Peekaboo. Or put these tricks together to create a "Day in the Life of Rover" performance. He starts the day with a big stretch (Downward Dog, page 74) and an Upward Dog (page 74). He plays golf (page 140) or baseball (page 134), then hide-and-seek. Once he's tired, he Goes to his Place (page 53), says his prayers (page 76) and tucks himself in (variation on Tuck Another Dog In, page 108)!

STEP-BY-STEP

1. Set up something for your dog to hide behind, such as a table on its side.

2. Throw a treat behind the table and tell him, "Fetch, go hide" (Fetch, page 31). Praise him for going behind the table.

3. Point to the table, toss the treat behind it and say, "go hide." Keep practicing, slowly weaning him off treats and just using praise. Then move onto other objects, such as a tree or picnic table.

4. You can stop the training here or transition to having him hide behind another person. Last but not least, teach him to hide behind you.

5. Practice three to five times a day for five to seven days.

 ADVICE FROM THE EXPERT

Make sure your dog is good at Stay (page 11) before you teach this trick. The concept of Stay while out of sight is advanced and even more so when you're out of *his* sight.

PROBLEM SOLVING

Problem: Your dog moves behind you, but then immediately comes back in front of you.

Solution: Break the trick down into individual parts. Make sure Rover knows Go out of the Room (page 116) and feels comfortable being out of your line of vision. He should also be comfortable being left alone. This is something you can teach by tying him outside a store and leaving him with a trusted friend.

★ ACKNOWLEDGMENTS ★

Babette: This book had so many moving parts and of all my years training and writing about dogs, I never worked harder in my life. However, the people who worked behind the scenes and allowed me the opportunity to work with their dogs worked even more tirelessly, and this never would have come to fruition if it had not been for their hard work and selfless dedication to this project. Carol Benjamin was one of my first role models when it came to teaching dogs tricks and writing a book. Bob Maida, one of my closest confidants and mentors who had some great ideas to include. Steve Diller has always been one to give me great feedback. Terry Haskins and Jesse Dalton who helped me find dogs that could do the work we needed for the book. Tamara Lee-Sang for her amazing photography. Will Kiester for his timeless patience and calm presence. My co-author Barbara Call who kept me focused and on track. The Page Street Team for all of the behind the scenes hours of labor of love they contributed.

Northern New Jersey German Shepherd Dog Club who allowed me to use their equipment and space. Pastor Bill and the Ramapo Reformed Church in Mahwah, New Jersey who allowed us to use their space on Sundays and even before the crack of dawn. Nikki Ostrower and Kirby, Megan Messina and Annie, Eddie and Linda Bocchino of the Woof Gang Bakery in Allendale, New Jersey, Nancy Scott and Calia. I can't thank Dawn Wolfe, Hope and Nikki enough. Dawn is and always has been a true friend through and through in all of our years of friendship.

Kellar's Canine Academy and Jodi Kellar for the use of their facility. Karen Profenna and her once-in-a-lifetime dog, Hailey who was willing to shoot before dawn on a Monday morning and then some. Karen and Hailey are an amazing team and a pleasure to know. Donna Van Ry and Carly. Tom and Judy Smith and Hana. Austin and Jamie Berkelhammer and Sebi. Candace Ball and Toshi San. Kristen Zimmerman and her awesome German Shepherd, Xanya.

Three amazing trainers who continue to do great things with their dogs and work as a tremendous team: Renee Shriver and Oscar; Rachel Stintzcum and Frazier; Martha Windisch with Spring, Sobey, Clue and Ghetty. Leslie GIordano and Mazie, David Fung and Bodhi. For Helene Cimaglia, the endless help that only a true friend can give.

Pat Muldowney, for all of his love and support both personally and professionally, along with Stevie. My fairy Godmother, Auntie, who has always been there and always will be. The kids and I would be lost without you. We love you. And most of all, Ryan and Sarah, every moment that I am training dogs is one less mommy moment and you understand. You both are the light and love of my life. I adore you both!

Barbara: Assembling *The Best Dog Tricks on the Planet* required the talents of many people. Generous thanks to my co-author Babette Haggerty for serving up plate after plate of canine knowledge, wisdom and advice—especially early in the morning and late at night. Many thanks to my publisher Will Kiester for bringing Babette and me together—I'll never forget that first phone call where you asked, "Barb, do you like dogs?" And many, many thanks to my compatriots at Page Street Publishing, as well as the talented freelance staff, for your expert guidance and assistance in bringing this book to life. Last but not least, thanks to Alex, Jack and Cody for never letting me forget how precious life is.

★ ABOUT THE AUTHORS ★

Babette Haggerty learned about square roots from her Golden Retriever, Muffin. Babette was six at the time and her dad was teaching Muffin how to add, subtract and find the square root. This was in the 1970's when most people didn't take their dogs to training class. Her television and movie work with dogs includes "All My Children", "The Guiding Light" and commercials for Black and Decker and AT&T. She even taught Jimmy Buffet's dog to dance to Margaritaville. Babette's proudest moment teaching dogs was when she surprised golfing great, Jack Nicklaus by teaching his Golden Retriever Cali to bark how many times his owner won the Masters. After spending 18 years training Palm Beach dogs, Babette has now returned to her native Bergen County where she shares her home with her two children, German Shepherd, French Bulldog, Norfolk Terrier and rescued Corgi.

Barbara R. Call is a professional writer, editor and artist who has written about everything from healthy cooking and sports to robotics and electrofusion. She is the author of six books, including *The Crafter's Devotional: 365 Tips, Tricks and Techniques for Unlocking Your Creative Spirit* (Quarry Books, 2008), and has ghostwritten, edited, copyedited and proofread dozens of other titles. She lives in North Andover, MA, with her two sons, Alex and Jack, and her rat terrier Cody.

★ INDEX ★